Can you rewrite old, negative thought patterns to change your future scripts? Instead of feeling trapped in the cycle of fear, can you break out of helplessness and move your life forward?

The answer is a resounding yes. You can do it. That's not to say it's easy. It's not. But you're worth it. You *can* learn better coping mechanisms that free you from feeling caged and hopeless. You can meet and deal with your fears in a spirit of openness and adventure. You can ask for guidance in living each moment to the best of your abilities.

We hope some of the ideas and techniques presented in *Creating Choices* will give you more options, more good raw materials for your new self. With more options comes a greater sense of personal empowerment and responsibility. And with a sense of personal empowerment and responsibility comes the ultimate joy of freedom—the freedom to create a life that fulfills your dreams.

D0913447

CREATING CHOICES

How Adult Children Can Turn Today's Dreams Into Tomorrow's Reality

Sheila Bayle-Lissick
and
Elise Marquam Jahns

A Hazelden Book
BALLANTINE BOOKS • NEW YORK

Editor's note:

Hazelden Educational Materials offers a variety of information on chemical dependency and related areas. Our publications do not necessarily represent Hazelden or its programs, nor do they officially speak for any Twelve Step organization.

Some of the stories of people in this book are based on the lives of actual people; some are composites based on the experiences of several people. In all cases, names have been changed and, in many cases, circumstances have been changed, to protect anonymity.

The following publishers have generously given permission to use extended quotes from copyrighted works: From *Minding the Body, Mending the Mind*, by Joan Borysenko, Ph.D. Copyright 1987 by Joan Borysenko, Ph.D. Reprinted with permission of Addison-Wesley Publishing Co., Inc., Reading, Massachusetts. From *The Power of Purpose*, by Richard J. Leider. Reprinted by permission of Ballantine Books. From *Imagineering: How to Profit from Your Creative Powers*, by Michael LeBoeuf. Published by Berkley Books. Reprinted by permission of McGraw-Hill Publishing Company. From *Prospering Woman*, by Ruth Ross, Ph.D. Reprinted by permission of New World Library, San Rafael, California. From *Release Your Brakes!* by James W. Newman: Reprinted by permission of James W. Newman.

Material from Susan Fowler-Woodring's seminar on ''Goal-Setting'' is reprinted with permission of CareerTrack Company, Boulder, Colo. (1-800-334-6780).

Library of Congress Catalog Card Number: 89-85502

ISBN 0-345-37378-2

This edition published by arrangement with Hazelden Foundation

Manufactured in the United States of America

First Ballantine Books Edition: September 1991

Dedication

To those who have helped me learn how to love and be loved: Joyce A., Sheila, Betty, Joyce W., Dave, and Liz.

To my family—who have offered loving support. And to Steve and Lorena—whose gifts of gentleness and love touch my soul daily.

—Elise

With thanks to my family, especially to my brothers, my husband Mark; Cindy; Roger; David; Susan; Elise; Sharon; Mike E.; Mike Z.; Beatrice; Jane; Elaine; Jolane; and my father, with love.

—Sheila

Contents

Dedication

Preface

Introduction: Goals for This Book................................. 1

Part One: Foundations of Change
1. Resources for Recovery 7
2. Reclaiming Your Sense of Spirituality 24
3. Developing Purpose....................................... 31
4. Developing Your Goal-Setting Process.................. 48
5. Developing Self-Esteem and Self-Worth................ 56
6. Taking Responsibility for Ourselves—Putting
   Ourselves First 66
7. Coping with High Expectations 71
8. Handling ''Slippery'' Situations 75
9. Cultivating a Sense of Commitment..................... 79
10. Designing Your Reward System 83

Part Two: The Process of Creating Choices
11. How the Process Can Work for You 91
12. Learning to Trust Your Intuition 96
13. Mindfulness: Creating an Attitude of Joy.............. 101
14. Learning to Ask for What You Want 104
15. Practicing How to Ask for What You Want 110
16. Trusting in the Outcome................................. 114
17. Understanding and Appreciating Synchronicity....... 119

Part Three: Activities
18. Introduction to Guidance Mechanisms 133
19. Energizing Yourself Through Exercise 138
20. Understanding and Using Subliminal Techniques ... 142
21. Using Relaxation Exercises, Guided Imagery, and
    Meditation 148

22. Incorporating Visualization Techniques into
    Your Life 154
23. Using Affirmations to Break Old Patterns 161
24. Journaling as a Tool for Release and Discovery 169

Part Four: Recovery at Work
25. Adult Children in the Workplace 175
26. Honing Your Decision-Making Skills 200

Part Five: Hanging in There
27. The Art of Persistence 213

Epilogue 217
Endnotes 219
Select Bibliography 221
Index 223

Preface

Think for a moment of a lump of clay. It is soft, cool, gray, and easily "moldable." It is smooth to the touch and can be shaped into any number of things. Each of us has probably molded a lump of clay into a vase, basket, ashtray, or other simple object. Though we may not have been experts at clay molding, we plunged in and took a risk. Perhaps we were not entirely pleased with the shape we had created, so we rolled it back into a ball and started the molding and building process again.

Each choice and decision in our life is like that lump of clay. We can shape our life in any number of ways. We can work with it steadily and meticulously, or quickly and decisively. We can let it sit for a while and contemplate which shape to mold it into. We can look at other shapes and finished pieces to get ideas and inspiration. If we're not quite ready to build the shape we want, we can choose to think about it further and hold off any action until we are thoroughly ready. This book is about learning how and when to mold our lives, and when to sit back and learn more about the process.

In 1986, the authors were sitting around talking about a class we had created, titled "Creating Choices: Getting What You Want." In the previous year, we had become good friends through talking about our mutual issues as adult children of alcoholics and had regularly gotten together to discuss the latest self-help books we had read and seminars we had attended. Elise was already teaching English courses part-time at a community college and suggested that the two of us create a class, utilizing much of the information we had been talking about. We did, and the class, which is about career and life-planning skills, found acceptance among a large group of students.

After teaching the class several times, we both began to feel a sense of frustration about the books we were using as suggested texts. Though the books were excellent resources on a variety of subjects, they didn't address several critical issues in ways that were useful to us; in other words, they weren't particularly good clay. So we decided it was time to write a book of our own, which we started molding.

We would get together one night a week and talk about what was happening in the classes. We discussed which ideas and exercises the students seemed to find helpful or frustrating. We started to see patterns that seemed to emerge in their lives: behavior changes and setting goals for the future. We also began to sense how change occurred in our own lives and how parallel some of our experiences were. But there was still a sense that something was missing, either in the outline of the chapters we had decided on for the book or in our approach as both teachers and students of the subjects with which we were grappling. We needed more raw materials but weren't sure how or when to add them or what the final mixture should be. We continued to refine our ideas until one other critical piece emerged from the lumps.

Both of us had discovered our interest in career- and life-planning ideas because of our focus on recovery in our own lives. Since both of us are adult children, it was the pain of our backgrounds that pushed us to deal with the problems we were encountering as adults. After several years in recovery, we began to seek ideas focusing on creating our futures.

Like most people in recovery, we had spent much time and effort healing the pain of the past and looking at ways to deal with our reactive, "survival model" behaviors. But when the time came to begin to live the kind of lives that we wanted to live, we weren't sure what they were. So we went on a discovery tour both individually and together and found lots of great ideas—new clay—about what it means to be an adult child. But we found very little on what to do after a person has been in recovery for several years and wants to move forward and stop focusing on the past. The old molds weren't useful any more, so we created our own, patterning them after our own experiences and that of many of our friends. This was the "actual piece" that had been missing.

Just as the final clay shape doesn't just appear, our lives don't just magically "happen." We have learned to choose rather than react. Though most of us won't be able to choose how we die, all of us choose how we are going to live. Fears may surface along the way, but we also have choices of how to deal with those fears. We may not know the direction to head next, but we can seek the guidance from our spiritual source. We can choose—both literally and metaphorically—healthy, nourishing food over the fast food that gives us only temporary satisfaction. We can learn to find good raw materials and allow the shapes and patterns to emerge from the darkness. This book is about learning to recognize the raw materials and actions that we need to mold our lives into the stuff of dreams.

There are several ideas that we hope our readers will find here: first, recovery can be a joyful and fulfilling ongoing focus; second, balance among the various aspects of our lives is key to our emotional well-being; third, no matter how difficult a childhood you had, you can build a future as bright and wonderful as you can imagine.

The authors aren't "experts" in the traditional sense. Many books on the market geared toward adult children are written by psychologists and medical doctors. Many of them are excellent and written by competent, caring professionals. We have read many of those books, and, in some cases, you will find them quoted. But in some sense, only you can know what activities or ideas will help you change your current situation and create your future. So no matter how many experts say that a particular kind of activity is the answer to a problem, please follow your own heart. We really are our own best experts, our own Michelangelos as it were.

Our thanks to Rebecca Post, our editor, whose expertise, patience, and enthusiasm buoyed us through the labyrinth of

writing this book. Thanks also to Maureen Bromenschenkel
whose patience and computer skills were important to this effort. We are also grateful to you, our readers, and hope that
some of the ideas in Creating Choices will bring you the joy
and hope that all people, adult children or otherwise, deserve.

Introduction

GOALS FOR THIS BOOK

From this book, we hope you will be able to obtain skills that will enable you to relax and clear your mind of "thought" clutter. You will gain these skills by participating in the activities offered in Part III. We also hope you will be able to set and work toward manageable goals—personal and professional—while reducing the effects of stress in your life. In doing so, you will be able to more clearly identify your objectives regarding your career, relationships, education, lifestyle, personal growth, spirituality, finances—whatever you choose to focus your time and attention on.

Some of our goals in writing *Creating Choices* have included:

- helping you develop a sense of empowerment and mastery over your life.
- offering you a "smorgasbord" of tools, ideas, and methods to help you create a sense of empowerment and mastery.
- teaching you what we know about setting reasonable and purposeful goals for your future, and how to develop manageable timetables for reaching those goals.
- offering you ideas about networking and support systems to assist you along the way. Also, we will let you know that you aren't alone—that there are many of us who understand what a struggle for belonging and a sense of well-being can feel like. Together, we will persevere on the road toward

1

wholeness and appreciate each other's company along the
way.
• helping you develop a feeling of closeness to yourself and
attain a sense of connectedness to the world and all its
myriad facets.
• helping you find a sense of balance between your work relationships and personal needs.

The above list is a tall order for any book—and we understand that personal growth is always a *process* and not an end
point at which you arrive, and then click into maintenance
mode. It just doesn't happen that way. But as you become
clearer about who you are and what you want, the process will
become more automatic. Rather than switch into some inappropriate survival skill mode which many of us learned as children, we can choose to act in ways that are appropriate and
unique, to our personal needs.

Most of what you will need to put into *Creating Choices* is
willingness: your willingness to try new things, your willingness to try and even fail at times in achieving goals you've set.
Perhaps even tougher than not achieving a particular goal is
having the willingness to push right to the brink—and over
"the other side" to success. Self-sabotage is a subtle and cun-
ning habit to break, but it is necessary to do so in attaining
success. A willingness to accept the outcome whether you succeed or fail is also important, as is the willingness to be open-
minded and persistent.

No self-help book in the world can help any of us unless we
are willing to try the ideas suggested and persist in doing the
activities often enough to discover what works for us—and what
doesn't. Sometimes you'll need to suspend judgment and let
the rational, logical part of your mind be silent. Activities such
as meditation and visualization discussed in Part III lend themselves to neither simple explanation nor predictable outcomes.
But many of you will find that these activities can help you.
You may feel relaxed, feel clearer mentally, be able to make
decisions quickly, and be more aware of your feelings and
needs. But you might not be able to draw straight line conclu-

sions as to what *exactly* brought about the changes for you. It's the old idea of being willing to Act As If.

Be Patient—Changes Take Time

Please also be patient and loving with yourself and your process. Changes take time and effort. If you have a habit you'd like to break but you've been practicing it for twenty years, how long will it take before you can reasonably expect to affect it? A month? Six months? A year? The hardest part, you may find, is doing anything long enough to actually see the changes occurring right before your eyes!

You will also need to live with occasional boredom and frustration. Repeatedly doing anything, particularly daily, will likely become boring after a while. Musicians, salespeople, research scientists, parents—most of us know how boring practically doing anything on a daily basis can be, especially if we don't like to do it. Whatever reward system you can create to support you through the dull times, you are encouraged to do. Remember, though, that if the rewards are fattening, expensive, or irresponsible in some way, they won't help your cause. If you want to design a positive reward system, Chapter Ten in this book can help.

You are strongly encouraged to find a support system of friends and programs that will nourish, nurture, and cheer your process of growth and change. It cannot be stated too strongly that learning about and having healthy relationships is not only what this book is about, but what we as humans are about. Some of us used to make relationships the unhealthy focus of all our energy; in this book, we're not talking about that. We're talking about balance among our many life pursuits. Strong, healthy, loving relationships are one way to learn about ourselves and where we are going. We'll discuss more about support systems in later chapters.

Having a Sense of Humor Really Helps

Finally, we'll ask you to think about cultivating a sense of humor. There seems to be no more serious group of humans than adult children. Put us in a room together and we can tell painful, sad, angry, and sometimes tragic stories until the wee hours of the morning with an intensity that is sometimes frightening. Many of us are less able than other people to stop in the middle of "one of those days" and laugh because it's all so ridiculous and out of our control.

Please think about ways to lighten up and enjoy yourself. You will have days when your child falls and tears her new outfit . . . when your boss points out what you didn't do in your staff meeting (even though you generated the agenda because he or she didn't have time) . . . when your mother-in-law calls and begs you not to be late for dinner, and you have a flat tire on the way to her house . . . and when you remember that you again forgot to take out the garbage that morning—for the third week in a row.

Call up a friend and laugh yourself weary about how unbelievable your day was and how glad you are that it's over. We can almost guarantee that you will feel little frustration and less anger about it the next day.

Problems are solved more smoothly when you don't "pack the angry garbage bag" with more stuff and cart it around with you. And your family and friends will appreciate your lighter attitude and good coping skills. If American writer Norman Cousins can use laughter to help cure himself of a disease, we can use it to beat a couple cases of the "woe is me." We might even find that some things aren't worth being serious about.

PART ONE

Foundations of Change

CHAPTER ONE

███

Resources for Recovery

Mary's Story

After showing up intoxicated for work one night, I was given an ultimatum.

Mary is a fifty-year-old mother, housewife, and former nurse. Her husband is an engineer who often works fifty-five-hour weeks, and they have two teenagers still living at home. Both of Mary's parents died in a car accident five years earlier; both were alcoholics and had been drinking the night the accident occurred.

"My recovery began in earnest about six months after the death of my parents," Mary recalls. "I was working as a nurse, suffering from intense depression, had gained a lot of weight since the accident, often chose to call in sick to work, and found myself yelling at my kids and fighting with my husband. I looked and felt miserable and began drinking to help ease the pain. After showing up intoxicated for work one night, I was given an ultimatum: either see a psychiatrist for a minimum of three months to figure out what was going on, or I would be fired. I chose the psychiatrist."

One of the first things the psychiatrist recommended was a thorough physical to which Mary agreed. "I found out that I was, not surprisingly, suffering from hypertension and a high cholesterol level. The first problems to deal with were my weight and tension level."

Mary knew that when it came to exercise, she had little motivation, and even knew that she was a good candidate for a heart attack. She had read in a hospital newsletter that the hospital had a walking club in its wellness clinic, and she literally walked out of her physician's office and into the wellness clinic and signed up. She was assigned a walking "buddy" and started exercising the very next day. Though it was difficult at first to keep her commitment—three times a week seemed like a lot—after the first few weeks she settled into a routine and found it became a habit.

"After three months of weekly sessions with the psychiatrist, I had identified several other problem areas. The first was my general overall schedule. Like most nurses, I worked rotating shifts, but even when I worked at night, I still tried to act like a supermom-wife. I finally screwed up my courage and hired a person to clean house for me every other week. Then I began to turn over some of the cooking and laundry chores to my children and husband. I admit that I almost gave up at this point because my family rebelled strongly at having to cook their own meals and care for their own clothing. There were bitter fights over 'Mom's selfishness,' but deep down I knew that my health was at stake. With the support of my psychiatrist and my walking buddy, I just kept chipping away at my old 'I can do it all' habits and, sure enough, a year later, even my youngest teenager could cook his own dinner on occasion. A major hurdle had been overcome."

Today, five years later, Mary continues to get better and better. She still walks but now it's as much as ten miles a week. She also swims on occasion and has started doing low-impact aerobics once a week for variety. During her year of seeing the psychiatrist, she discovered that her childhood in an alcoholic family affected her deeply. Mary has since found books very helpful to her and has joined a book discussion club. She quit her job to go back to school and is working on her master's degree in nursing. For the past twenty-five years, Mary had wanted to go back to school but could never find the courage to do so until she saw how important it was to take care of *her* health as well as her family's. Since she has gained so much from her own study of adult children of alcoholics, she is seriously considering working in a chemical dependency center when she is done with school. Mary and her husband, Greg, still have all of the problems and issues that they had five years ago, but they have new coping mechanisms with which to deal with them.

So for Mary the process was:

- choosing self-care and health as being of *primary* importance.
- finding support for her new way of living.
- being willing to take risks and standing behind her choices.
- continuing to learn what she can about alcoholism.
- sticking with the basics for the long-term—for Mary that's exercise and assertiveness.

The Process of Recovery

Once you start a path of recovery, it seems to become easier and easier to find ways of supporting your desires to find healthy ways of living. This chapter is filled with ideas and options that many people use as practical tools. Sometimes it is necessary to try many techniques before finding those that feel comfortable and "right." We have read many books. Sometimes only portions of these books have been useful. But it was necessary to read these, then sift out the helpful parts. We could then combine pieces and parts of the readings and integrate the information into our lives as circumstances warranted.

Before we go any further, we'll reiterate that recovery is a *process*, not a goal. Goals and objectives are very much a part of recovery, but experience tells us that we won't suddenly stop one day, realize that we're perfectly happy, and then just work, play, and live at that level. But we will cease, at some point, thinking of ourselves as being in recovery and move on to focusing more and more energy into growing as a person; this is what Abraham Maslow, a widely published psychologist, describes as *self-actualizing*. There's no definition of what that will look like or feel like. But self-actualized people know when what they're doing feels good and produces positive changes. They enjoy the path they've chosen and want to stay with it. It is our hope that you will find useful options in the resources described in this chapter, but not necessarily final answers.

Avoid Rigid Thinking

Rigid thinking is common in alcoholic families. Sometimes it seems that our brain waves literally find grooved patterns of negativity and won't move or change without tremendous effort. For years we may have had thoughts like: *Well, I will try this new group (or meditation technique, book, herbalist, yoga exercise, subliminal tape, et cetera) and then I will be fine. This is really the method that is going to make me better and will cure my negative thinking (or insecurity, low self-esteem, nail biting, moodiness, financial problems, et cetera).* Beware of thinking like this. No one book or relaxation technique has been the sole answer to a behavior pattern change. The benefits of any one technique or process tend to enhance other techniques and build on previous successes, rather than prove to be answers in and of themselves.

As always, think about what you want, do your research, strive to keep an open mind, be willing to experiment with new options, and keep checking your goals and expectations for outcomes. Think "flexibility" and "possibility" instead of "must-have-or-die" rigidity. One more thing—have fun!

Join a Support Group

The most obvious first option is a support group of some kind: Al-Anon, a Twelve Step adult children of alcoholics group, church, spirituality groups, a book discussion club, or once-a-month potluck dinners with like-minded people.

Knowing other people who are working on similar issues and

whom you can call regularly is the foundation of a solid recovery program. In Chapter Two on spirituality, we make references to a sense of connectedness being important to nurturing spirituality and a sense of self. Groups are really a focal point of feeling connected. Many of us felt isolated and helpless when we were growing up; we learned to rely on ourselves and only ourselves, not trusting others to be there for us when we needed them. Connecting to a group, or to at least two or three other people, begins the process of breaking down the walls of disappointment and mistrust that we may have built. We can begin to clearly see that we aren't alone anymore, that there are others who not only understand who we really are but who are often willing to help us and love us. Camaraderie and a sense of belonging can help deepen and enrich the process of recovery.

If You Live in a Rural Area Where Few Group Options Exist . . .

Try to find two or three people with whom you can be totally honest and who are also interested in growth and change. Think about contacting your local public health office to find out what options exist in terms of support groups for families of alcoholics, or look in your phone book for an Alcoholics Anonymous (AA) listing. Even if there isn't an Al-Anon or adult children's group listed, someone in an AA group may know of an Al-Anon meeting in a neighboring town or know of other people who are interested in starting a group.

If you live in a remote area, you might already understand how hard it can be to remain in regular contact with people other than your immediate family. Telephone calls, shortwave radio messages, or letters are among your options; some people even find a pen pal in an adult child group in the nearest metropolitan area. Use your imagination and try to do what you can, but do figure out ways to stay in touch with other recovering people.

If You Live in a Metropolitan Area . . .

Here, you might have more of a problem because there might be an overwhelming number of options to pursue. Start with a

Twelve Step group or other self-help programs and make that an anchor point. Then think about the other needs and interests you have and look into the possibilities. Certain disciplines in psychology offer therapy groups as both treatment aftercare and as ongoing programs with a structured environment in which to pursue changes in behavior. Ask your therapist, if you have one, whether group therapy might be appropriate for you. Beware that, as with most programs facilitated by a professional, group therapy can be costly and might not be covered by health insurance.

When Seeking Professional Help . . .

Some states have certain standards, credential requirements, and licensing procedures in order to use the title *psychologist* or *counselor*. In other states, there aren't any requirements or few minimal standards to be met, so essentially almost anyone can hang out a sign and become a practicing therapist. It takes assertive shopping to find the right person in the right setting.

The best option is probably to ask other adult children you know for referrals to professionals they have found helpful. There are also professional associations able and willing to make referrals to psychologists. Check the Yellow Pages of your telephone directory under "Psychologist." If you live in a metropolitan area, the chances are excellent that there will be a referral service in the city. The referral service can refer you to someone who specializes in the treatment of adult children of alcoholics or who has expertise in the dynamics of alcoholic families.

If you live in a rural or remote area, check the Yellow Pages under the same heading, since most states have statewide referral services. If your state does not, contact either the state or local public health department, and ask for assistance in finding resources for families of alcoholics. Every state has a public health department, as do most counties. Many county public health clinics will already have some expertise in delivering health services in rural or remote areas and might be an excellent source of ideas on how to stay in touch with other people in recovery programs.

Develop Other Recovery Resources

After you have established or reestablished an anchor point for your recovery program, begin thinking about what other information or assistance you might want. Also think about how much time, energy, and money you want to spend. For some people, a group is all they want or need. For others, it is important to have a group, one or two close friends, a spiritual discipline such as t'ai chi or yoga, a religious community to which they belong, and sufficient resources to attend seminars, workshops, and retreats regularly. Still others are content to read a book once in a while, have one or two close friends, and attend an occasional workshop. The journey is a personal one, and you are in the best position to decide where your interests are and how much time you are willing to spend.

The rest of this chapter describes several paths that people have created for themselves as they developed their resources for recovery. See if you can discover something useful in their journeys that you can incorporate into your own recovery process.

Larry's Story

Something was working for these people, and I wanted to find out what it was.

For Larry the process has been somewhat different. A high school dropout at fifteen, Larry found trouble at every turn.

Larry recalls, "My father was a rageful, cruel, violent alcoholic. He would beat my brothers and me at the slightest provocation. He also sexually abused my sister, though I didn't know that at the time. My mother was a quiet, timid woman. She worked long, hard hours at a local laundromat and at home she said very little even when my dad gave me a concussion one day because I had forgotten to pick up the mail on my way home from school. I was eight at the time."

Larry asked his AA sponsor, Mike, a question about what Mike had done to learn more about relationships. Mike mentioned that he attended an Al-Anon meeting, and explained what he thought the differences were between the two programs (AA and Al-Anon). He also told Larry about adult children Twelve Step meetings. Larry called the local intergroup office and got a meeting schedule. He attended several different Al-Anon and adult children meetings to see what they were about.

"I found myself feeling most comfortable in an adult children meeting that I found. I attended regularly and though I often felt that I wasn't getting it, I was determined to stick to it. It was obvious to me that others in the group had found healthy ways to be in relationships and not feel crazy, lonely, or both. Something was working for these people, and I wanted to find out what it was."

Larry says he learned something important about himself and about his recovery after almost a year in an adult child group. People in his regular meeting and people in other groups were talking a lot about books they had read, lectures they had attended, workshops they wanted to attend, or speakers they wanted to hear. They seemed able to organize all the information in a way that was useful to them. Whenever Larry listened to them talk, he felt overwhelmed and frustrated. Though he was able to read and often enjoyed it, he felt that he wasn't learning enough by simply reading books. He said not enough of what he was reading was sinking in, and he was overwhelmed by the number of books available.

"I somehow realized along the way that what I really wanted was a sponsor. I wanted to be able to make sense with someone about this 'relationship stuff.' I wanted someone who could help me by being available to talk with me regularly, probably once a week. I knew that my AA sponsor had been the cornerstone of my recovery in that program, and I figured maybe having a sponsor in my adult child group would help me in the same way. I called several people on the phone list from my group. Finally, I found a man I felt I could make a good connection with. Two years later, that decision is still working."

For Larry, the most important aspects of his recovery are:

- finding an adult child group and focusing on that.
- getting a sponsor in that program, someone with whom he can regularly talk one-on-one.
- staying with what he knows. Larry had to set limits about trying outside activities, such as going to workshops or reading books. If his friends want to do those things, that's okay with Larry. But he is no longer willing to push himself to do things that might "be good for him" that he doesn't enjoy. Larry is aware that his "limits" may change in the future.
- learning what he can about the effects growing up in an alcoholic family can have on relationship skills.
- choosing, for now, to learn how to be friends with several women, hoping that he will later be able to deepen a relationship from friendship to love.
- taking the time he needs to get to know himself better, finding out what he wants in a relationship, and developing self-confidence and self-esteem in himself as a potential partner or spouse.

Larry's recovery program is really geared toward relationships rather than covering a broad, confusing spectrum of personal issues. His choice is very much a reflection of the slogan, Keep It Simple.

Jim's Story

After eight months of unrelenting pressure at home and at work, I finally just snapped.

Jim is a middle manager in a Fortune 500 manufacturing company. He is thirty-eight, married, has children ages six, ten, and twelve, and shares the responsibility of caring for his alcoholic mother who is suffering from heart disease. She lives just a couple miles away.

Jim started his recovery four years ago after a very stressful period. "First, my mother had fallen and broken a hip," he recalls. "It was the fifth trip to the hospital for her in two years for falls that resulted in broken bones. Her recuperation was long and difficult, resulting in lots of additional work for me in taking care of her and the home she lived in. Finally, I had to face her drinking problem and talk with my brothers and sisters about whether to commit her to treatment.''

The second crisis occurred two weeks after Jim's mother fell. His youngest child, a son named Justin, was diagnosed as having a heart ailment that would require several surgeries. Not only would there be financial pressures because of the additional medical bills, but Jim was frightened that Justin might die.

"My father had died while undergoing coronary bypass surgery when I was sixteen. I don't think I ever really grieved my father's death. And I was terrified of hospitals and doctors. The prospect of my son undergoing open heart surgery terrified me, but I didn't know what other choice there was."

The third problem was the situation in Jim's company. Because of financial problems, Jim's company was laying off hundreds of people in an attempt to prevent either bankruptcy or a takeover. For months there were constant rumors about what was going to happen in Jim's division, particularly his position. He worked fifty-five- and sixty-hour weeks, trying to hang on to his job and the positions of the people who worked for him.

"After eight months of unrelenting pressure at home and work, I finally just snapped. One Friday evening at work, I walked into another manager's office, and he asked me how I was doing. I began to relate just a few of the things that were going on, trying to make jokes about it, but found myself starting to cry. Don listened quietly as I told my story of stress, anguish, fear, frustration, and exhaustion. A half hour later, almost unable to move because I was so tired, I listened as Don called employee assistance and requested an appointment for me with the company psychologist the following week.''

Don drove Jim home that night and told Jim's wife, Sue, what had happened. Don suggested that she accompany Jim to his appointment the following Monday. It was a turning point for Jim and his whole family.

The employee assistance psychologist, after hearing the story, suggested therapy for Jim and his wife and referred them to a local clinic. Though very reluctant to spend time and money on "some damn shrink," Jim finally agreed to go after Sue threatened to leave him unless he went to counseling with her. She had been under as much pressure as Jim. It was time for outside help.

Jim and Sue went to counseling together for eight months. Then, at the suggestion of the therapist, Jim, Sue, and their children went through family therapy at a local treatment center for chemical dependency and codependency. Jim's mother started the program with them but dropped out after just two weeks. Jim, Sue, and their children finished without her. They recognized that it was extremely important for them to learn how to deal with the disease of alcoholism.

"After treatment, I joined an aftercare group that was geared toward dealing with men's issues," Jim says. "I still attend those meetings. Though I went to Al-Anon for a while, I don't want to spend two evenings a week away from my family. I'll return to Al-Anon when I'm finished with my men's group therapy, if I feel the need."

In the meantime, Jim says he relates strongly to the men in the group who, like him, are mostly professionals. Some of them are married, all of them have children, and all of them come from alcoholic families.

"I finally feel like I have found a safe, supportive environment, which helps me make decisions and grow. Not surprisingly, I discovered that Don, my associate at work whose office I had 'crashed' in, was a graduate of this group and is also a recovering adult child of an alcoholic. I feel fortunate to know of another male manager in my company whose counsel I can seek when other avenues of help seem unsafe or unavailable to me."

For Jim, the recovery plan is:

• attend weekly men's group meetings.
• take occasional mini-vacations with his family.

Until something else "changes" in Jim's schedule, he will stay with his support group and his occasional getaways with his family or by himself. He has learned, sometimes the hard way, to set strict limits for himself in terms of outside commitments. He practices asking for help a lot. He doesn't feel the need to act like the strong one anymore. And though his mother continues to drink and her health continues to decline, Jim knows he has choices about whether or not to be involved with her life. When he needs to reserve his strength for himself or for Sue or his children, he does so. He would be the first to say that the hardest work he does is to take care of himself. He is most grateful for his aftercare group because of their support of his healthy new behaviors and emphasis on learning new self-care habits.

Mary Pat's Story
. . . if I could make myself throw up, I didn't gain any weight from the food.

A thirty-five-year-old Ph.D. in computer science, Mary Pat is a consultant in software design. A genius in creating graphics software for engineering design work, Mary Pat has experienced incredible success at work. She is a recovering bulimic in addition to being an adult child of an alcoholic. She works hard at setting limits on the number of hours she works because of a strong tendency to be compulsive about working. She is engaged to a man who is a lawyer in a small firm that he helped found.

"My childhood was spent trotting around the globe with my parents, both of whom were research doctors for a major American university," she recalls. "My strongest memories are of the nannies who cared for me and who could never speak English. By the time I was seven, I could speak three languages fluently, and understood two more well enough to attend local schools when they were available. My other memory of childhood is of being lonely, isolated, and usually left to the care of people other than my parents.

"At sixteen, I was sent back to the United States to attend college. I was obviously much younger than most of my classmates and withdrew behind a wall of work and food. But still, I was always the top student in my class. I often stayed up all night studying. In order to stay awake, I first tried caffeine and speed. After a while, though, I discovered that sugar was a much better stimulant for me. I also discovered that if I could make myself throw up, I didn't gain any weight from the food. In my mind, looking back on that period of my life, I feel I was using food in an unhealthy way from early childhood. But I didn't really feel the effects until I was living away from my parents' home.''

Mary Pat graduated at nineteen with a bachelor of science degree in computer science and went straight into graduate school. At twenty-two, she fell in love with a fellow graduate student, and they started living together very soon after meeting. Within months, it became obvious to Rick that Mary Pat had an eating disorder, and he tried to convince her to see a doctor or enter treatment. For almost two years, they argued about her health. Finally Rick decided to leave the relationship. When Mary Pat realized that Rick wasn't coming back, she attempted suicide. She was found and brought to the hospital in time to save her life.

Mary Pat committed herself to an eating disorders treatment program while still in the hospital. She also joined Overeaters Anonymous (OA) and slowly began to emerge from the shell she had crawled into so many years before. After three years in OA, though, she began to feel restless and unhappy again about her life. She decided to go back into therapy.

''After several months in therapy, at the recommendation of my therapist, I also joined Al-Anon. Though I knew that my father was an alcoholic, I really hadn't given it much thought. There were so many other issues from my childhood that were painful, I hadn't separated out the fact that my father's alcoholism might be important for me to deal with. When I finally made the connection that my father's illness was part of my present problems, I realized that I had a new point to focus on and move from. This time the point to focus on wasn't as much about my primary addiction as it was about my behaviors in relationships. I felt very grateful to have been able to identify the source of the restlessness and pain in my life again.''

With her customary energy and focus, Mary Pat set out to learn everything she could about what it meant to be an adult child of an alcoholic. She continued to attend Al-Anon meetings. She also attended lectures on adult child issues offered by several local treatment centers. She read many books, including Janet Woititz's *Adult Children of Alcoholics* and Claudia Black's *It Will Never Happen to Me*. She went on retreats, she took journaling workshops, she learned about dream interpretation, and she started meditating. She learned t'ai chi and took sailing lessons. She discovered books on holistic health and began to change her eating and work habits. She found tremendous intellectual stimulation and satisfaction in fully immersing herself in the study of new, healthy ways of living that would help her heal old wounds and create new ways of being. She continued on this track for three years.

At the end of the three-year period, she started to reduce the time she spent studying recovery techniques so she could redirect her energy to creating a consulting business. Mary Pat had become very aware, during her three years working an intensive recovery program, of just how much she craved time to engage in her favorite activities, such as sailing and meditating. She was working in a large corporation at the time and often had deadlines that created long workweeks with little free time. She was tired of working fifty-five- and sixty-hour weeks and delaying her vacations to get her job done. Unfortunately, before she could get her business plan finished, her boss found out that she was planning to leave and transferred her to another division. She was so unhappy in her new position that she decided to leave the company earlier than planned.

"Though I had assumed that I would enjoy my new freedom and independence, I became so depressed about being without a job that I began to stay in bed all day. I returned to eating habits that were unhealthy for me and stopped exercising and going to meetings. For the first time in my life, I was without either the structure or reward system that first my studies and then my work had provided for me. Though my friends called me regularly trying to convince me to go to meetings or go back to therapy, I kept putting them off. When I began to feel desperate and afraid, I decided to call my therapist and try, once more, to figure out a way to deal with my 'monsters.' I made an appointment for the following week.''

Mary Pat's story of ''falling off the wagon'' is included here because most of us fall away from our recovery programs at one time or another. Sometimes we become bored with how normal and stable our lives become. So we try to create some excitement, negative or positive. Some of us choose to become involved in unhealthy relationships. Others choose to think that they have recovered completely, only to find out several months later that they aren't yet able to handle their problems or behaviors without a set program and help from others who understand them. Sometimes we find ourselves in changing situations, as Mary Pat did. Even when they are of our own choosing, such changes may knock us off our path hard enough that we have trouble recovering our equilibrium, let alone our direction. In some ways, though, Mary Pat never left her recovery program. She needed to fall down one more time to learn another piece about her childhood that would allow her to make additional adjustments. Some of us learn better the hard way!

Mary Pat stayed in therapy for about six months. She realized through this period that she was just beginning to truly know who she was and what she wanted for herself when she left her job. Unfortunately for her, she had so identified with her work that when she lost her job, she felt she had lost her identity. She had finally discovered what was for her the last big piece of her recovery: to no longer tie her self-esteem to how much work she produced in a week.

Five years later, Mary Pat is an immensely successful consultant who travels all over the world doing her work. Since she travels so much, Mary Pat has learned to keep her program simple and easy so she can ''carry'' it with her wherever she goes. The following program works for her:

- She attends Al-Anon once a week. If she is out of town, she finds a meeting to go to wherever she happens to be.
- She has asked her travel agent to find hotels that have exercise facilities. She also calls ahead to ask for special foods

so that she isn't tempted to eat things she knows aren't good for her.

- She carries a portable Walkman-style tape player and several meditation tapes to listen to regularly.

- She makes arrangements to go sailing whenever possible. Sailing reminds her that a basic premise of her recovery is to mix fun in with her work. She no longer is embarrassed about taking an afternoon off to take a sailing lesson and has found that several of her clients are thrilled to be invited to go along. It has been a lifesaver as a social event as opposed to always going out to dinner or to a cocktail party.

- Mary Pat carries her address book with phone numbers wherever she goes. She calls home regularly but also knows when it is time to call someone because she's feeling disconnected, lonely, or afraid. If she can't reach anyone, she calls a special number at her home that has a tape-recorded message with the voices of her fiancé and several friends. It is a bright, cheerful message about how much she is loved, appreciated, and missed. Mary Pat likes listening to these messages so much she records a different message every other month. It is both a lifeline and a reminder of how hard she works her self-care program.

Mary Pat has enjoyed ten years in recovery for both her primary addiction and her relationship and behavior issues. She is both joyful and grateful to have found a way to really live with her upbringing and everything that goes with that.

Areas to Focus Attention

In the following section, we have listed some of the criteria that Mary, Larry, Jim, and Mary Pat used in making decisions about their recovery program. Though these criteria may be useful to you, this is by no means meant to be a comprehensive or rigid list. If you have any other considerations, by all means add them.

- The connection to a group of like-minded people or several individuals.
- The need or timing of professional assistance—treatment, therapy, or group therapy.
- The amount of resources you have available to dedicate to recovery. The three biggest to consider are time, energy, and money. Learning when to say yes and when to say no are a big part of recovery for most of us. Our own recovery programs are a great place to practice!
- The need to assess responsibilities or previous commitments to yourself, your spouse, children, parents, or other family members, work, home and car repair, volunteer community service, and your religious community. Most of us have busy lives already. Can you really afford to add activities to your current schedules? Are there times you can afford not to?
- The attention to learning. Ask yourself: *How will I best absorb new information? From classes, seminars, books, other people, tapes, videotapes, or other means?* Today, an attractive variety of learning tools and options are available for us to use in recovery. Some of them are discussed in this book.

It's important to experiment and find the learning style that works best for you. For example, if you are often attending lectures, but your learning style is best suited to doing instead of listening, you may not absorb as much information as you'd like. A therapy group where you can role-play might be more useful. So ask yourself what you like best—listening, reading, or doing. Or perhaps you prefer a combination of activities. Once you've decided, keep that information in mind as you think about activities to support your recovery.

CHAPTER TWO

||||||||||||||||||||||||||||||||||||||||||||||||||||||||||||||||||||||||||||||||||

Reclaiming Your Sense of Spirituality

Most self-help books that deal with recovering from growing up in a dysfunctional family talk about spirituality. You can find definitions for it, explanations of what it is, and rational outlines of how to be more spiritual. Many of the chapters in this book are designed, in fact, to help you become more spiritual. So what is spirituality?

Right now, get out a piece of paper and a pen or pencil. Put the word *Spirituality* at the top of the page. Then write your own definition of spirituality, what it means to you, how you practice your spirituality, and what effect these spiritual practices have on your life. Please close this book and write your *own* explanation of spirituality. This isn't a test. No one else is going to know whether you decided to do this or not, and certainly no one needs to ever see your writing. You are entitled to privacy at all times on this or any other issue or idea you are working on. Please write the definition for yourself, so that you have a working definition of what spirituality means to you as you read the rest of this chapter and book. It will help you make sense of this somewhat nebulous idea. Go ahead now, take ten minutes and write as much as you can.

What Spirituality Means

Now that you managed to write a definition, build on this definition over time. You were asked to do this to make the point that spirituality is very much an individual idea or journey. If you were able to compare your definition with a half dozen other people's, you would find similarities. But even using the exact same methods to nurture your spirituality such as meditation, exercise, journaling, and visualization, you would still arrive at different conclusions. Why? Well, let's try to define spirituality first.

Connectedness

For the authors, *spirituality* means a sense of connectedness, centeredness, and purpose. Many people work on their spiritual self to feel connected to their world—work, home, family—and to their Higher Power or God. Some people don't hold a traditional religious or dogmatic viewpoint of what God is. They've redefined their concept of a Higher Power so that they're not tapping into an old guilt and shame from childhood. The best definition of *God*—for many people—is the one found in the Twelve Steps: "a Power greater than ourselves." Finding a working definition of God is part of the spiritual journey they engage in when they choose recovery as their path. They finally admitted they weren't able to make themselves well— they needed help—and lots of it. This is the core of many people's spirituality—that they need help and want to feel connected to themselves and to the world.

Think about this for a minute. How many of our problems as adult children stem from loneliness, anger, fear, and isolation? Probably a large percentage. How can we begin to overcome our loneliness, anger, fear, and isolation? We can choose to become connected by engaging in activities that reinforce our connections and connectedness to the God of our understanding and to the people with whom we choose to share our lives. Love and friendship form the foundation of connections to people. Love and prayer form the foundation of connections to a Higher Power. So the first part of our spirituality equation is *connectedness*.

Centeredness

The second part of spirituality is *centeredness*—a feeling of knowing who we are and what we want and staying with our self—particularly when the path we're on becomes uneven or just plain rough. For example, in recovery many of us learn that we're people-pleaser types. It's something we can be neither proud of, nor ashamed of, but our tendency is to do what others want in a situation rather than what we want. When we first start recovery, others may tell us that this tendency puts us in the position of "giving power away." We walked away from situations for years feeling as though we had been ripped off, but then we hear someone telling us that we're "giving it away."

Sarah's Story

I got to know myself and found a center.

Sarah explains how her self-defeating behavior was related to her spirituality issues. "With the mind-set of a zealot on a pilgrimage, I determined that this was just a habit of mine, this people-pleasing stuff, and I could break it. I tried many things: talking to my therapist, reading books about assertiveness, rehearsing what I would say in certain situations, and talking with friends about how they would handle themselves under similar circumstances. I did this for the best part of a couple of years and made good progress in trying not to give my power away.

"The underlying problem for me at the time, though, was that I kept trying to stop what I perceived to be a bad habit [people-pleasing] in many instances without knowing what I actually wanted. I was still reacting to other people by saying no instead of yes and still giving my power away much of the time.

"Somewhere along the way I received a blinding flash of the obvious. No, I didn't want to do things anymore to manipulate people into liking, loving, and accepting me. I had identified a problem in my life correctly and had further identified methods of helping cope with that problem. What needed attention then was the issue underlying my people-pleasing habit—a lack of a sense of self. I was just beginning to realize that saying *yes* or *no* wasn't the whole issue—discovering what I wanted to do and *then* backing myself up was.''

Sarah, like many of us, began to realize that her questions were closely related to her centeredness and spirituality. ''About seven years ago I took my focus away from trying to simply break a bad habit and turned my attention inward. I began to remember to ask myself questions like: *What do I want from this situation? What do I need here? Are* yes *and* no *the only answers to the question or can I find a middle ground? Am I willing to accept responsibility for my decision? What do I do if the outcome is negative?* I began to really ask myself what I wanted and committed myself to listening to my inner voice and doing what I needed to move toward my desires. To put it simply—I got to know myself and found a center.''

In defining spirituality, we need to know where our center is, what nourishes us spiritually, and what we're willing to do under certain conditions such as feeling fatigued, hungry, frustrated, or lonely. By knowing who we are, what we want, and how we've coped with situations in the past, we act from a place of strength. This strength connects us to our spiritual self—our center. This feeling of being centered is nurtured often by really becoming connected and understanding what our purpose is—the third part of our definition.

Purpose
Purpose is not only knowing what we want but having a sense of direction in our lives. One of the most difficult parts of recovery can involve wrestling with the concept of purpose: *Why am I here, and how can I focus my talents and energy to reach toward what I want? How can I discover what my purpose really is?* We may long for a concrete, logical, linear

answer here, but one doesn't exist. Purpose is a quality that each of us has, but each of us is unique and must discover our purpose for ourselves. Purpose is found in the essence of our dreams, our fantasies, the work that we choose to perform, the friends we choose, and the homes we live in. It can be seen in the decisions we make and the directions we head, and most particularly, how we care for ourselves in good times and bad.

Many recovering people say one portion of their purpose in life is to learn good, high quality self-care practices and then use them consistently. They can attend to other aspects in their lives much better if they take care of themselves physically, emotionally, and mentally. Their lives flow over the rough spots rather than coming to an abrupt stop for hours or days. Because they have accepted self-care as a part of their purpose, they're often more able to see or sense the moments when other aspects of their purpose are being revealed in the course of daily events.

Developing Spirituality

After you have had a chance to define your sense of what spirituality is, think about what you do that supports your spirituality. What activities do you engage in to nurture your inner self? Do you find regular periods of quiet time in which to meditate or simply slow your mind's "chatter" after a busy day? Are you able to enjoy many of the everyday tasks that you perform as a matter of course? If you aren't, this is a very powerful message to you about what you are choosing to spend your time doing and whether or not it feeds your spirituality very well.

Developing spirituality doesn't mean we stop doing the mundane tasks of life. We all need to eat, wash clothes, pick up after ourselves, work for a living, parent our children and ourselves, and much more. But we need to think about why we are doing these things.

Learning to Live Mindfully

Try living for a week with a very conscious mind-set. Don't let your eyes glaze over and your brain waves go flat the next time you have to do something that you don't enjoy. The Buddhists call this concept *living mindfully*, and it is well worth the time and energy spent on it. (For more on mindfulness, see Chapter Thirteen, pages 101–103.) Take time to notice how you live, how you choose to spend your time, and then record some of your observations. You will probably learn a great deal about yourself—how centered or frazzled you are; how good it feels to restore order when you clear your desk top and file important papers; how much you love to see your children's creativity unfold as they fingerpaint and how much less irritating it is to clean up after them. How about the moments of peace and quiet when you sense your connection to the greater whole? How about actually hearing the birds in the morning when you are jogging?

The point of all this is that living mindfully reveals the minor details of our daily life in a deep way and can help us let go of thoughts of drudgery and frustration. Reclaiming our sense of spirituality can begin with seeing ourselves consciously going about daily living. Rather than simply trying to avoid certain tasks, we can immerse ourselves in them and see their connection to filling our needs and fulfilling our purpose. One of the greatest benefits in choosing to be mindful is a stronger link to small joys and less awareness of the negative ones. We'll feel less self-pity and live spiritually when we're conscious of our time and efforts. That is no small feat for those of us who grew up in an alcoholic family.

Listening to Our Inner Child

For many adult children, a big part of spirituality involves being attentive to our inner child, the little person who is the source of much inspiration, humor, and creativity. Sarah explains it this way: "When I'm in an adult mode, I'm usually acting responsibly toward my work, family, and friends. It can become a pattern with me to begin to ignore the voice inside me that begs for ice cream, that wants to go to the zoo, that needs a nap, or that wants to jump in a pile of leaves she's just helped rake. When I ignore her for weeks or months, I'm essentially treating her needs—and neediness—in the same way my parents treated me when I was a child. Now I've learned skills that allow me to treat myself differently. I don't need to shame myself for feeling needy or feel embarrassed to act joyfully, and a little silly, in public. I have learned self-acceptance and self-care for all the parts of me, and my inner child is an integral part of my psyche. I can no longer disown her or her behavior without becoming sick, depressed, or rageful.''

When we are attentive to our inner child, we are rewarded with creative energy, joy in the wonders of the world around us, confidence in our ability to handle things, and a sense of belonging. The time invested up front is more than worth the outcome, especially when it is, for many of us, such an essential part of feeling connected, centered, and full of purpose— in other words, spiritual.

We, the authors, hope that this discussion has helped you hone your definition of spirituality and that you can add to it over time. Make spirituality work for you, and the rewards will last a lifetime.

CHAPTER THREE

||||||||||||||||||||||||||||||||||||||||||||||||||||||||||||||||||||||

Developing Purpose

In the previous chapter, the last part of the definition on spirituality was about purpose: knowing what our purpose is in life and then seeking ways to fulfill it. It sounds so simple, but finding purpose in your life can be difficult and challenging. This chapter is designed to help you begin to ask questions such as, *Why am I here?* and *What do I want to do with my life?* Then, with the help of the exercises in some of the following sections of this book, you can begin to move beyond the questions to finding answers and finding ways to move toward your goals.

Determining What We Like to Do

Dan's friend, Dave, called to thank Dan for the book he'd sent—Marsha Sinetar's *Do What You Love, The Money Will Follow*. "But you know, Dan," he said, "the problem is I don't *know* what I want to do." Dan heard the frustration and anger in Dave's voice and understood. He'd experienced exactly the same frustration himself for a number of years.

Another friend of Dan's, Michael, related how he was talking with a counselor when he was going through his divorce. The counselor asked, "What do *you* like to do?" Michael sat in silence and felt some panic, realizing that he was supposed to have an answer, but he didn't. He was thirty-four years old and didn't know what he liked to do!

Why is it that so many of us adult children of alcoholics simply don't know what we like to do and what we want to do with our lives? We spent much of our childhood taking care of others or developing coping and survival strategies that enabled us to survive the emotionally and sometimes physically chaotic world of dysfunctional family life. Frequently, those coping mechanisms involved developing a highly attuned antenna system so we could react in a way that would keep us safe from emotional or physical hurt.

Since so much of our time was spent *reacting*, we weren't actively considering what *we* wanted, what *we* liked, what made *us* feel good or happy. Our needs frequently did not count or were ignored. We learned early that our needs wouldn't be met in a consistent or positive way, so we learned not to ask and programmed ourselves so we learned not to need. We learned to count on ourselves only, never asking for help or for what we needed or wanted. Since we've had years of practice ignoring our needs or feeling we didn't deserve good things in our lives, is it surprising that most of us *don't* know what we want or what makes us feel good?

To make this situation even more difficult, most of us probably believe privately that *everyone else* knows what they want and need; "they" seem to be forging ahead with their lives while we feel helpless and "at sea." The irony is that a great many other people don't know what they want either. But they won't admit it for a variety of reasons: they would feel silly or weak; they are "too old" or have too many responsibilities to make changes; they couldn't handle the criticism or discomfort from their family and friends.

On top of this factor, there's somehow a feeling that once we make a decision about what to do with our lives, we need to stick with that decision no matter what. It's somehow "weak" or "wrong" to change one's mind and life.

And let's make no mistake about it, such changes do pose threats to those close to us. It's not that our families and friends don't want what's best for us, but any change threatens their sense of comfort and security.

Perhaps you'll change so much that you won't want or need them. Perhaps your changes make them realize they aren't sure what they want either, and they're afraid and uncomfortable confronting that fact. Perhaps your change means that you'll have less time to give them and their needs won't be met. These are real issues, ones that will take courage, time, and communication skills to work through. That's why it's important to develop a support group of friends who will encourage you and support your positive change. (For more on support groups, refer back to the section in Chapter One called "Join a Support Group," pages 10–12.)

Finding a Sense of Direction

The questions now are

- *where do I start?* and
- *how do I find out what I want to do?*

It's a process that will involve some "aha insight," some "blinding glimpses of the obvious," some hard work and frustration, but it will be well worth the effort. A sense of direction focuses our energy, galvanizes our self-worth, and creates a feeling of inner joy and contentment. It's not so much the achievement of the goal that counts; it's the power, excitement, creativity, ingenuity, persistence, determination, and sense of worth and enthusiasm that are generated along the way. Having a sense of direction is a powerful, magnetic force that will attract other positive, enthusiastic, and motivated people into your life in seemingly unusual and bizarre ways.

Think back to a time in your life when you were extremely motivated to accomplish something. Perhaps it was finishing a needlepoint pillow for a special friend's birthday, saving enough money for a two-week dream vacation to Hawaii, or finishing a market study that could boost sales and result in a possible 10 percent raise. Obstacles to attaining these goals fell by the wayside—you found time and solutions because you had the energy, passion, and enthusiasm to make these goals happen. You were excited, alive, and working toward a goal that had meaning in your life.

Gail Sheehy, in her book *Pathfinders*, discusses the results of a three-year research study drawn from responses to sixty thousand questionnaires.[1] Sheehy also interviewed respondents by phone and in person. In her discussion of "The Ten Hallmarks of Well-Being," she notes that the one characteristic that correlates most closely to optimum life satisfaction is a person's ability to say, "My life has meaning and direction." These individuals have found meaning in an involvement with something beyond themselves—work, other people, social activism, an idea. Sheehy also contends that the inability of many Americans to find a sense of purpose in their work has fostered the shift from a work ethic in our society to a self-fulfillment ethic.

According to Richard Leider, author of *The Power of Purpose, purpose* means focusing on what deeply satisfies you. It means occupying yourself and your time with people, commitments, ideas, and challenges that help you feel worthwhile and make a difference.[2] Leider points out that in their bestselling book, *In Search of Excellence*, Thomas J. Peters and Robert H. Waterman, Jr., note that "people who perform most energetically, creatively, and enthusiastically are those who believe they are contributing to a purpose larger than themselves: in other words, they have a mission."[3]

Some people seem *born* to a sense of purpose—Pinchas Zukerman to music, Albert Einstein to mathematical genius. But what about the rest of us? Many of us know what we *don't* want in our lives—but how many of us have specific ideas of what we *do* want? Or perhaps we have many different interests. How do we decide which interest to pursue?

Leider believes that we have three hungers in our life:

1. The hunger for meaning: to have our lives recognized as worthwhile.

2. The hunger for intimacy and community: to be cared about and to give and receive love.
3. The hunger for self: to develop, grow, and decide how to most effectively utilize our talents during a short lifetime.[4]

We all need a dream worth dreaming—a dream worthy of our unique talents, gifts, skills, and enthusiasms. Dreams—or passions—affect our motivation, the way we go about doing things, decisions we make or don't make, and ultimately the degree of satisfaction and happiness with "who we are." We need to clarify and prioritize those dreams. We need to create the day-to-day small steps from which we can extract joy and pride in accomplishment. The accomplishment keeps us motivated and focused on the joy of the process, which is important in reaching our goal.

Once you know your purpose, it's relatively smooth sailing. The hardest part is answering the questions:

• What do I really want?
• What is my purpose?
• What do I really care about and what excites me?

Dr. Ruth Ross in her book *Prospering Woman* states that we are a composite of subpersonalities.[5] Different roles and different people bring out different facets of our personalities. At various times in your life, each of these roles can take on greater meaning or require more of a time commitment than at other times. For instance, after the birth of a baby, a husband and wife are more likely to spend most of their time with a "parenting" role than a "husband and wife" role. To determine the various subpersonalities residing within you, the various roles you play, and their importance to you, Ross suggests that you take a sheet of paper and pen or pencil and ask yourself, *Who am I?* Then jot down all the roles and personalities that are part of your life. Hint: Think of all the activities that crowd your day, and then determine what roles those activities might fulfill. For instance, you are in a "banker and investor" role when it comes to balancing your checkbook and investing money. When you just *have* to have an ice cream cone, your "kid" role is emerging. There may be twenty or thirty different roles that are part of your life. Jot down as many as you can.

After completing this list, review your roles and consider if any of them are in conflict. For instance, your "banker," who is intent on saving money, may be tugging against your "traveler/adventurer," who wants to spend two weeks in Portugal. Once you can pinpoint that the tug between these two roles is causing anxiety, you can brainstorm possible solutions. Can you still plan the trip but postpone it a while longer so you won't deplete your savings? Or, does it make more sense to reduce the amount you plan to save since taking that vacation ranks near the top of your priority list? It's frequently important to compromise so you can satisfy both major wants and bring some peace and balance into your life. The secret is to make sure that your major desires are satisfying most of the needs expressed through your subpersonalities.

Identifying Your Values

An important next step is to look at our values—values are strongly reflected in our work, our friends, how we choose to spend our time, and how we perceive situations. If our goals are out of sync with our values, this will thwart our energy and ability to reach our goals.

By answering the questions that follow, you can get a concrete sense of where your values are. There are no right or wrong answers—there are only answers that will lead you to a better understanding of what you truly want in life.

Do Your Goals Reflect Your Values?[6]

As we learn to utilize goal-setting to create desirable changes, we need to acknowledge our values. Wants that nourish us are built on values we hold dear. These values, through our belief systems, are unconsciously determining our behavior patterns at every moment. Yet, many of us cannot identify our values. Do you know what is important to you?

Look over the following quiz, and write your answers on a separate piece of paper. Let your answers to these questions stimulate you to think about values that are real for you. The origin of your values has long been unconscious, but just answering a few simple questions will quickly reveal personal preferences. Sharing answers with a friend is very helpful, too, especially as you bring out details in your discussion.

Values—being self-reliant, daring, logical, loving, polite, tidy, congruent, truthful, honest, capable, forgiving, responsible, self-controlled, open-minded, and so on—are only *implied* in our answers. We must look between the lines. Our values emerge in our choice of work, how we relate to people, how we spend our time, and how we think.

VALUES QUIZ[7]

I. Answer these four questions off the top of your head:

1. If you could do anything you wanted for one week, what would you do?
2. What three things do you want people to remember about you?
3. Finish this sentence: "Happiness is . . ."
4. What always makes you angry?

II. What is important to you in your personal relations and life experiences? Rate the following items on a scale of one to ten (one being lowly valued, ten being highly valued), and share with a friend *why* you rated each item the way you did.

A loving relationship _____
Being physically attractive _____
A satisfying marriage _____
Two months' vacation a year _____

A chance to be creative _____
Making a difference in the world _____
Freedom to make your own decisions _____
A beautiful home _____
Optimal health _____
Unlimited travel _____
Honesty with friends _____
Sensuous sex life _____
Your own large library _____
Peace in the world _____
To be treated fairly _____
Confidence in yourself _____
Influence and power in your community _____
High spiritual experience _____
A satisfying religious faith _____
Dependable transportation _____
Someone who needs you _____
Orderliness in your affairs _____
A close-knit family _____
Wealth _____
Other _____

III. What is important to you in your actual work conditions?
(Using the same rating system.)

To work alone _____
Regular hours and guaranteed pay _____
Totally unstructured workday _____
Self-employment _____
Good supervision _____
Having a variety of tasks _____
Work in a small organization _____
Outdoor work _____
Opportunity for overtime _____
Little responsibility and risks _____
Short commute _____
Other _____

If you marked two or three items as a "9" or "10" in each section, you will have a clear picture of the highest ranking values in your personal relations, life experiences, and work conditions. If you marked many items with a "9" or "10," you may want to put aside these pages for a while. When you return to the pages, check to see if you'd still mark the items in the same way. If so, you'll need to further prioritize all items you've marked "9" or "10."

Choose three things from the fourteen choices that follow that give you the most satisfaction in your work.
1. To be excited by what you're doing
2. To help others solve problems
3. To contribute to society with worthwhile work
4. To be recognized as an authority
5. To motivate yourself
6. To figure things out
7. To work within a structured situation
8. To think through new solutions
9. To have choice about time
10. To make a lot of money
11. To work in a team
12. To work out-of-doors
13. To be respected for your work
14. Other _____

Over the next few months, observe if your desires change. Do these new desires reflect a change in values? Values change very slowly. Although at the rational level we *decide* to be different, our automatic responses, based on old values, often prevail. As your goals and values become more congruent, you become more powerful, for then you are not in conflict with yourself.

WHAT DO I WANT?
SELF-DISCOVERY EXERCISES[8]

The closer we are to being the directors of our lives, the more in touch we feel with our dreams and desires. We need now to let go and daydream a little. It's very useful to establish a daily program of taking a few minutes to think, write, read, and meditate on goals. Some of these suggestions may help structure that time, which should be approached in an easy, relaxed manner.

Knowing What You Want

1. On a separate sheet of paper, list the major areas of your life such as love, home, work, play, health, finance, career, independence, travel, recreation, self-confidence building, personal growth, and relationships. Then write down what you want in each of these areas.

2. Ask yourself the following questions and keep a diary of your answers:

• List what you don't want.
• List what you "should want" according to the significant people in your life.
• What hasn't lived yet in your life?
• What have you always wanted to do some day?
• What would you do if you could do anything you wanted for a year?
• How much money would you like to be making a year from now? Five years from now?

3. Daydream a little. Long-hidden wants sometimes reveal themselves in intuitive flashes. They rarely show you the whole plan, or lay out your way like the yellow brick road. Ideas come and go quickly in the form of images. Write

them down. The dullest ink lasts longer than the sharpest memory.

4. Turn envious thoughts to positive use. When you feel envy at someone's good fortune, know that this may be a signal for some want you have. Release the envy and keep the desire.

5. Create an image of the ideal for yourself. Remember, it's good to desire; wanting is a prerequisite for receiving. How would you ideally have your life? Put on soft music, lie back, close your eyes, and imagine an entire day.

6. Learn to pick a "bouquet of roses" from the "thorn bushes" in your life. Inside every dissatisfaction is a want. When you're experiencing any negative emotion, keep asking yourself, *What do I want?* Avoid the inclination to just remain upset. Remind yourself that the world is yours for the asking—but you must know exactly what you want.

Questions to Ask Yourself

What you have been doing so far is creating prosperity goals in general terms. Before the goals become specific, they need to survive a series of other questions. Observe your intentions and reactions as you ask yourself:

- Have I dared to think big enough?
- Is my goal based on pure fantasy?
- Is it achievable, believable, and measurable?
- Is the goal life-producing?
- Does it hurt others?
- Does this goal really belong to others?
- Is it legal?
- Is it good for all concerned?
- Do I have the consciousness of having this goal?
- Can I see myself already having it?
- Have I investigated what I will need to do to reach this goal (such as education, experience)?

- Am I willing to undertake the undesirable aspects of the job in question?
- Can I handle the rewards of getting this goal?
- Am I willing to take on the responsibility of this goal?

At first, tell no one about your desires. Later, you may want feedback about how others see your project, but when you are initially building your confidence and accepting your own decisions as valuable, give your ideas time to germinate. Getting a negative response from others too soon might cause you to release your desires prematurely. You do not want to put yourself in a position of explaining or justifying your desires and ideas while they are still fresh and new to you. Let them develop a strength of their own before you share them.

Tapping into Your Past Life: Areas that Brought Inner Joy

In order to discover our true purpose, many of us need to "unearth" the passions, hopes, and dreams that we buried long ago. This "unearthing" process may not come quickly or easily if we sit down and logically analyze our thoughts, but they can bubble to the surface if we access our right brain capabilities—those capabilities associated with imagery, intuition, and feelings. Since these passions, hopes, and dreams have been deeply buried with layers of phrases such as *I should . . . I have to . . . I must be responsible . . . I need to be practical . . . I ought to . . . I just can't . . . I'd better not . . .* we need to tap into a process that will penetrate these layers and reach our essence, our uniqueness, our deepest self.

To do this, we will guide you through a process that will put you in touch with your true self. You will journey through your early life and reconnect with your inner child in a healthy, fulfilling way. You will remember the activities, interests, thoughts, playtimes, games and experiences that brought you a sense of joy, that absorbed you completely, fascinated you, and lifted you beyond the ordinary into the extraordinary. Once you get in touch with your inner child and release your fantasies, buried dreams, and passions, you may have valuable clues and insights that can tell you about your true desires and what you love. It is at this point that you can decide how you can incorporate what you love into your daily life to bring you greater richness and enjoyment. You can also take one or two specific areas of your life that you wish to concentrate on (for example, spiritual, financial, physical, career, or relationships) and apply what you've discovered about your inner child.

Once you have completed these following exercises, you can then share what you've learned about yourself with a trusted friend. Ask for feedback. What clarity, ideas, or insights does your friend bring to your discovery journey?

Getting in Touch with Your Favorite Place

The first step necessary to access your right brain is to relax. Sit or lie in a comfortable place. Wear comfortable, loose clothing, and play your favorite relaxation music.

Breathe deeply—in through your nose and out through your mouth. Repeat this deep breath process several times, and then imagine your favorite place. It could be an imagined meadow or mountaintop . . . a white sand beach with the sound of gentle, lapping waves . . . a tree fort hideaway . . . a pine-scented forest filled with the echoes of bird calls.

Whatever that favorite spot of yours is, be there completely— physically, mentally, and emotionally.

Live your experience fully by enjoying it through all your senses. Hear the song of birds . . . the rustling of pines . . . the soft, repetitious lapping of waves . . . see the color and texture of wildflowers in the meadow . . . feel the soft, cool breezes . . . taste the salty ocean air . . . touch the flow of the waves, the softness of the wildflower petal. Live the experience completely and fully with your entire being. Let yourself see . . . hear . . . taste . . . touch . . . feel the experience.

Now picture yourself as a five year old who is completely free to do what you love most.

- Are you fingerpainting?
- Playing in the leaves?
- Inventing an imaginary friend?
- Building models?

Let yourself truly be five years old again.

- What are you most enjoying?
- Where are you?
- Are you alone or with others?
- If you're with others, are these people strangers or friends?
- Where do you like to go?
- What do you most like doing with your best friend?
- What do you enjoy doing with your grandparents?
- What do you like when you visit other places?
- What favorite things do you remember from trips you've taken?
- What do you collect?
- What do your friends do that you really would love to do?
- Who do you most admire, and why?
- Who do you dream about being when you grow up?

All of these thoughts trigger memories of delight and pleasure and give you clues about who you are. This will aid you in your present self-discovery process.

Now repeat the same process, but visualize yourself at the age of ten, then sixteen, and finally twenty-one.

After completing these exercises, write down your memories and thoughts at all ages, or speak into a tape recorder. Record as fully as possible all the things that brought you pleasure at each age.

Applying What You've Learned

The next step is to determine how these activities, loves, and passions might fit into your life now. What do they tell you about your career desires, the management style or environment you feel most comfortable with? Do you prefer to be outdoors or indoors? Alone or with others? Concentrating on one project or on a variety of projects?

Next, concentrate on one or two areas of your life where you want to change—for example, in terms of finances, relationships, physical health, career, or spiritual development. Ask yourself *What part of me does*_____(fill in the blank with the activities or interests you discovered in your guided imagery journey) *help to nourish? What can I do to incorporate this activity into my life?*

Sharing What You've Learned with a Friend

After you've had the opportunity to review your responses and comments, you may wish to share your lists and ideas with a trusted friend. Ask for your friend's counsel and advice. What does he or she hear, perceive, or understand that you might have missed?

Tapping into the experiences, activities, and thoughts that brought inner joy at several different passages in your life can prove to be an extremely valuable source of knowledge. Things may pop out that you might never have expected. Some things may seem impractical or frivolous. But don't abandon any of these thoughts. Jot down all of them so you can review them periodically. When you begin to incorporate some of these loves and passions into your present life, you will not only empower yourself, but you will be further along on the road of recovery and much nearer to connecting with your sense of purpose in life. One last exercise that immediately follows can bring you even closer to that goal.

HOW TO DEVELOP YOUR LIFE PURPOSE STATEMENT[9]

Take a pen or pencil and a separate piece of paper and do the following exercise.

1. List your two most outstanding personal qualities. (These should be nouns. For instance, I am a good *listener* or I have *integrity*.)
2. List your two best methods of expressing yourself. (For instance, I express myself best through *writing, debating, speaking, nurturing*, etcetera.)
3. Define your idea of the perfect world.

STATEMENT OF PURPOSE
(Using above information)

My purpose is to use my _____ and _____ (answers to number 1 above) to express myself through _____ and _____ (answers to number 2 above) so that my world will be _____ (answer to number 3)

Perhaps you would like to put the statement into your own words, or add other information. If so, complete the following sentence:

My purpose in life is:
_____
_____
_____

You may have read through all of these exercises without actually taking the time to try them. Perhaps they seem too time-consuming or overwhelming. Or perhaps you wonder what good they could really do. After all, you are who you are; you have responsibilities in your life; there are certain things you just can't believe will change in your life.

But you deserve the time to find out more about *you*. Many of us adult children have been so busy trying to take care of the needs of others that we haven't let ourselves explore our own wants and needs. Or we haven't known how to go about it. For example, consider John. He simply didn't *know* what he liked to do. That frustrated him, but it also turned on a giant light bulb in his head. He decided to give himself time to figure out what he *did* like. And it *did* take time, but he gradually came to realize how much he enjoyed riding a motorcycle and learning to play the guitar.

So give yourself space and time to write out answers to these exercises. You may be surprised by what pops into your head. Although some flashes may not seem practical or relevant, be sure to record all your thoughts. Such flashes may not seem practical at the moment, but they can give you a clue into your innermost being that can be valuable. Or, that seemingly "irrelevant" thought can be valuable six months or a year later.

There's no doubt about it—determining our wants, desires, and sense of purpose can be hard work. But it's worth it and we deserve it. One of the reasons it may be especially hard for some of us adult children is that we've spent much of our lives *reacting* to others and trying to determine others' needs rather than our own. And that behavior was, in many cases, very necessary for our physical and emotional survival.

But those patterns may no longer serve us well. We may need to spend time focusing on *us*—focusing on who we are, what we want, and where we're going. As we do this, we'll begin to feel a greater sense of energy and peace. As we become the best that we can be and work toward recognizing and fulfilling the magnificent potential that we have, we begin to function from an inner sense of self-knowledge that may translate to others and ourselves as self-confidence. Ironically, as we gain a greater sense of self-confidence, we're better able to meet our needs, and that helps us to better meet the needs of those we most love.

CHAPTER FOUR

██

Developing Your Goal-Setting Process

Once you determine your wants and needs, you can start thinking about what it will take to get your needs met so you can fulfill your purpose. Your current focus may be on recovery, or it may be on other issues. In either case, good goal-setting skills will allow you to focus your energy and organize your activities to serve your goals rather than detract from them. This is where you start focusing on getting what you want.

Do you find it hard to believe that only 5 percent of Americans set goals and only 1 percent of Americans write down those goals? Most of us spend more time planning our vacations than planning where we want to go with our lives.

But major research studies confirm the importance of setting goals. Separate studies at Harvard University, Massachusetts Institute of Technology, and Cornell University report similar findings: every peak-performing person is motivated by goals.

A 1952 study of Yale University graduates found that 3 percent had set goals. In a follow-up study twenty years later, it was found that the 3 percent who had set goals achieved more than the other 97 percent of graduates combined!

James W. Newman in his book, *Release Your Brakes!* relates a story about the long, lazy drives his family would take when he was a child.[1] More than once they ended up lost. As they meandered along, no one would pay any attention to road markers until one of the kids would cry out, "Hey, I'm hungry; let's go home." All of a sudden, all eyes would focus on road signs so they could find their way back home quickly.

And that's how it works. When your goal and focus become very clear, you notice the road signs that you didn't pay the least bit of attention to earlier. Similarly, when you have a clearly defined goal structure, opportunities that will help you to meet those goals are more readily apparent. As Dr. Michael LeBoeuf, Ph.D., states in his book, *Imagineering*, "One of the most amazing things to me is the way that new ideas and opportunities come to those who decide what they want and have the courage to pursue it. It's the closest thing to real magic I know of."[2]

People are by nature goal-directed. If you doubt this, think for a moment of those individuals you know or you've heard about who retire but haven't made plans for the period following their retirement. Statistics bear out that the mortality rate for these individuals is substantially higher than for those who have made plans. Think also of the amazing, almost superhuman, goal-directed activity that occurred between 1960 and 1970 after President John F. Kennedy set a goal for landing an American on the moon. What seemed like an impossible mission in 1960 became a reality in 1969. Never before in the history of the space program had such ideas, hard work, and effort been marshalled. The combination of many people putting forth almost a superhuman effort to achieve a national goal produced the desired result.

Think also of a time when there was something in your life that you really wanted—whether it was taking a vacation, buying your first car, or learning to ride a bike. Can you recall the energy and excitement you generated to meet that goal? Just thinking about it creates positive momentum and a sense of accomplishment and well-being, doesn't it? That reaction creates a positive cycle "snowball" effect that can lead you to more success. Dr. LeBoeuf has termed this cycle the "Success Cycle" which is illustrated here.[3]

Success Cycle

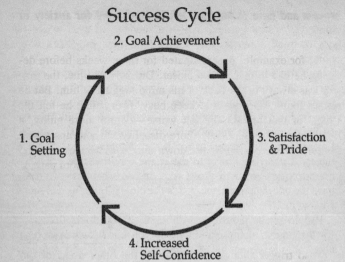

2. Goal Achievement

1. Goal
Setting

3. Satisfaction
& Pride

4. Increased
Self-Confidence

Once you begin to achieve goals, you feel a sense of pride and satisfaction in your accomplishments. As a result, you are more likely to set and reach new goals. These series of successes create greater self-reliance and self-trust, which enhance your capacity to reach for and achieve even larger goals. And, not surprisingly, with your positive belief comes a certain sense of serenity and peace of mind. This also increases your chances for success.

Taking Action Makes the Difference

Have you ever noticed that when you worry about an upcoming project or delay its start, it becomes harder and harder to begin the project? But once you actually start the project, it doesn't seem nearly as difficult or overwhelming as you had imagined. Once action is taken, you become absorbed in that process and have little room left in your mind for anxiety or worry.

Joe, for example, procrastinated for three weeks before deciding he had to clean out a closet. During that time, the project was always in the back of his mind tugging at him. But he always found other ways to keep busy. Every time he felt the "tug" of that project, he felt worse—a little more guilty, a little more anxious, a little more disappointed and upset with himself. When he finally sat down amidst the boxes, opened the first one and started sorting through old high school papers, he really became immersed in the project.

We've all probably had experiences like Joe's. When we're feeling overwhelmed or very anxious, action can be very positive, productive, and energizing—a real mobilizing force that can also trigger thought action about the other areas of our lives.

For instance, as you're going through old papers, a certain photo might remind you to call a person in the photo for his or her opinion on a problem you've been wrestling with.

If goal setting results in major achievements and accomplishments as borne out by research, and if goal setting serves to enhance the "Success Cycle," why do so few of us actually do it? We're masters at coming up with reasons why we can't do things. We all have our favorite ways of avoiding goal setting. That small voice of negativity cries out in full force: *It takes too much time, and I just have too many other responsibilities. Or what if I don't reach the goal? What if I fail? What if I set my expectations too high and then fall on my face? Friends, relatives, children, and others will be there with the "I told you so" refrain.*

There's no getting around it—change is hard. But once you decide that goals can make a difference in your life, you'll find the time, energy, and support you need. It's a matter of deciding that you deserve the success that setting goals will bring.

The Biggest Risk of All . . .

One of the most interesting games we play with goal setting involves our thoughts and attitudes about risk taking. But, if you think about it, the greatest risk is not to take a risk—to always wonder what "might have been." We may also have the idea that not taking risks brings security into our lives. But take a moment and think about what Helen Keller, the late American lecturer who was deaf and blind, said: "Security is mostly a superstition. It does not exist in nature, nor do the children of men as a whole experience it. Avoiding danger in the long run is no safer than outright exposure. Life is either a daring adventure or nothing."

One man who is a real believer in goal setting once shared the following quote, which he kept tucked away in the desk drawer in his office: "The worst thing one can do is not to try; to be aware of what one wants and not give in to it; to spend years in silent hurt wondering if something could have materialized—and never knowing."

GOAL-SETTING EXERCISES

Since strong desire and enthusiasm are important components in achieving your goals, it's important to select the two or three goals that are most important to you.

But where do you begin? Dr. LeBoeuf suggests the following method:[4]

First, take index cards or sheets of paper and jot down one of the following goal heading categories on each sheet or card:

- Career Goals
- Financial Goals
- Personal/Relationship Goals
- Physical Goals
- Personal Growth/Spiritual Goals
- Social/Recreational Goals

Prioritizing Goals

Quickly, without taking time to censor or analyze, write down a list of goals on each of these cards. Write down as many as you can: at least three in each area. After completing this exercise for all six goal areas, go back and pick the two most important goals in each of the six categories. Now, on a separate sheet or card, list these twelve goals.

The next step is to further narrow and define your true wants. From this list of twelve, choose your three most important goals—the ones that excite you the most, that generate passion, that you feel most strongly about—that would make your life richer, fuller, and more joyful. Delete any and all goals that smack of "I should . . ." or "parents, children, spouse, significant other, employer think I should . . ." Remember, these are *your* goals and passions. Now prioritize these goals.

Goals need to be put in writing to reinforce your commitment to them. They also need to be as specific as possible. Rather than saying you want to be financially independent, indicate the amount of money you wish to have and the specific steps you will take each month that will lead to financial independence. For instance, "I will save or invest $_____ per month."

Are the Goals Realistic?

Also make sure your goals are compatible and not mutually exclusive. For instance, if you want to take a cruise in January for your vacation but also want to save one thousand dollars by January, can both be accomplished? If not, decide which is the more important goal and work toward accomplishing that goal.

Remember, Goals Are Not Carved in Stone

Also keep in mind that goals are not carved in stone. You may change your mind about what's most important to you, depending on other things that are occurring in your life. Just remain flexible and feel perfectly fine making adjustments. Goals provide an important framework, but they must also accommodate growth and change.

Set Deadlines

Another key factor in goal setting is to set a time frame for each goal—daily goals, short-term goals (less than a year), and long-range goals. Deadlines enable us to focus on our goals and pace ourselves accordingly. Also remember the Pareto Principle (also commonly known as the 80/20 Rule): 80 percent of your accomplishments result from meeting 20 percent of your goals.

Imagine the Goal Is Reached

Remind yourself of your goals frequently. Perhaps you'll want to put your goal list on the refrigerator, the mirror of your bathroom, by your telephone, or by your bedside table. And, very importantly, take ten minutes each day to visualize yourself achieving your goals. Use all your senses and experience fully the attainment of your goal. If one of your most important goals is a Caribbean vacation, feel the sand between your toes on the beach; hear the sound of the surf; smell the salt water and suntan lotion, see the palm trees; and taste a dinner of freshly caught fish.

Setting a goal is like using a magnifying glass to direct and concentrate the rays of the sun to produce a fire. It's a way to focus your energies and enthusiasm toward a want or passion that's truly significant for you and you alone.

Not only will setting goals help you get where you want to go more quickly and easily, but the process will also have many important side benefits. Since immobilization is a cause, not a result, of depression, it's hard to be fully involved in pursuing an important goal and to be depressed at the same time.[5] Also, as you take action to achieve a goal, you are giving your life more meaning. And many researchers have concluded that one of the most important factors in maintaining good mental *and* physical health is having a sense of meaning and purpose in life.

Remember, as you picture yourself achieving your goals, you will be increasing your *expectancy* of achieving your goals. And as you increase your *expectancy* of achieving your goals, you will begin to automatically act in ways that will contribute to your ability to achieve your goals.

To achieve anything truly worthwhile, you must know clearly what you want, you must deeply want it, and you must intend to get it. Keep clearly before you the picture of what you want to be, and you'll begin to truly experience the magical powers of goal setting.

CHAPTER FIVE

||||||||||||||||||||||||||||||||||||||||||||||||||||||||||||||||||||||||||||

Developing Self-Esteem
And Self-Worth

Many of the activities in this book are designed to help create and support self-esteem and self-worth. By focusing on developing purpose, creating goals, and nurturing goal-setting skills, we are creating inner changes in our psyches that support self-worth and self-esteem. But often our "self-talk" doesn't reflect the changes we are trying to create elsewhere in our lives. The following stories offer scenarios that, for some, may sound all too familiar.

Sarah walked by Gwen's desk and was surprised to hear her saying to herself: *You dummy, how could you do that?* Sarah asked her what had happened, and Gwen replied: "I can't believe how stupid I was. I put two letters in the mail that had three typos in them. Just imagine if they had gone out? I called the mail room, and they found them and sent them back to me—but what a dummy!" For the next three or four minutes, Gwen continued to shake her head and tell herself what "an idiot" she'd been.

Jim walked in the front door slowly. It was a hot July afternoon, but he wasn't thinking about the heat. He'd just been laid off his job. He and his wife and three children had moved to this town only three years ago, and it had taken him six months to land an assembly job in one of the factories. Because he was a "new hire," he knew that if things got tight for the company, he'd be one of the first to go. But he'd tried to shut that possibility out of his mind. After all, it couldn't happen for a second time, could it? That's why they'd moved to this town in the first place—to get a fresh start. Instead, he was out of work again. Why had he thought a new town would make a difference? He just wasn't any good. He never made the right decision, and his whole family would have to suffer because of his stupidity. How could he face his wife? He sat at the kitchen table with his face in his hands—tired and depressed.

Jean felt devastated. A man she'd been seeing for over a year had just called her to wish her a happy birthday and then said, "I'll call you sometime." Of course, he never did. That was his way of ending the relationship. The relationship had been rocky for nearly four months, but she had no idea what had really happened between them. She kept asking herself, *What did I do wrong?* Over the next few months she was deeply depressed. She analyzed past conversations word by word, wondering what she could have said to be more interesting or how she could have been more fun to be with. No matter what portion of the relationship she viewed, she always came up short. *Obviously*, she thought, *something was wrong with her if this man had left.*

All of us face life situations from time to time that may play havoc with our self-esteem. But the higher our self-esteem, the more quickly we can accept the "valleys" in our life and return to an equilibrium. When we have a strong sense of self-esteem, we are comfortable and happy with who we are as human beings. We look inward and experience a sense of contentment and a sense that on the deepest level, we're "okay."

Stopping the Cycle of Negative Thinking

How we feel about ourselves not only affects our attitudes. It also affects how we approach our day-to-day living, the risks we take (or don't take), the awareness we have of our thoughts and actions, and our ability to accept responsibility for them. With a healthy sense of self-esteem, we can easily bounce back from setbacks. We can be more creative in our work and our play and be optimistic about what we hope life will bring us. If we have a good sense of self-esteem, we're also more likely to convey a sense of ease about ourselves and a sense of respect toward others. Self-esteem affects our relationships and the sense of serenity and peacefulness we experience in our day-to-day living.

So much of what we feel about ourselves results from what we *tell* ourselves. When we begin to use negative words or phrases, we start a cycle of negative thinking, frequently conjuring up thoughts of other "stupid" or "dumb" things we've done. It's very important to be aware of this pattern and to consciously call a halt to it. And we *can* call a halt to it. Some people find it useful to simply say "stop" out loud and picture a big red stop sign.

One man uses an image that you may find especially powerful. When he finds himself in a negative thought mode, he pictures a huge, wooden door with iron reinforcements—one that might have been found in a medieval castle. He pictures that heavy, massive door slamming shut with an echo which reverberates through the entire structure. The sounds, visual image, and the smell of this image serve as a strong reminder to him. If these images don't evoke a particularly strong or powerful response for you, choose an image of your own that will very solidly imprint the concept "stop" in your mind.

Replace Negative Thoughts with Positive Affirmations

Once you've called a halt to these negative thoughts, then what? Try replacing the negative thoughts with positive affirmations about particular strengths that you have such as: *I am a kind, considerate person*, or *I'm fun to be with*, or *I am bright and articulate*. You may want to repeat these statements out loud a number of times and then write them out or read them into a tape recorder and then listen to them. (For more on affirmations, see Chapter Twenty-Three, "Using Affirmations to Break Old Patterns," pages 161–168.)

Another technique you might try is writing down all the things you like about yourself or listing your accomplishments—big and small. Or, another approach is listing all the things you've managed to accomplish in the past few days. Many of us have a tendency to dwell on what we *haven't* done rather than what we *have* done. No matter how many items we've crossed off our "to do" list, we seem to frequently focus on the two or three we *haven't* yet completed. But just look at what you *have* done and stop for a moment to give yourself a well-deserved, hearty, and sincere congratulations.

Consider Starting a Project

Once you've stopped the cycle of negative thinking and worked with your affirmations, it's time to move on to the next step. Consider starting a project you've had in mind—whether it's sweeping out the garage, reorganizing a closet, or writing letters. *What* the project is isn't important. What *is* important is starting in on it, getting absorbed in it, and feeling the sense of accomplishment that comes from working on the project.

The process of losing yourself in a project is part of the beneficial result of plunging into a task. You've experienced this before in your life when you've gotten involved in something you enjoyed doing and just lost track of time. Before you knew it, hours slipped by without your being aware of it.

If you think back to your school days, you may remember projects that seemed impossible at first, but once you got started the time flew by. Jack recalls such an example.

Jack's Story
I became completely absorbed in the drawing . . .

"The most vivid memory I have of such a feeling is from a drawing class several years ago. Our instructor informed us that for the next three class periods, three hours each, we would work on a pencil drawing of any part of the interior of our classroom building. After finding the part of the building I wished to sketch, I settled in to start the drawing. The thoughts that kept running through my mind were: *Three hours! How can I sit here and draw for three hours? I have laundry at home to do; I need to shop for a wedding present; I have to finish reading two short stories for my class.* I was agitated and irritated. But as I kept sketching, those initial thoughts faded. Before I was even aware of it, three hours had passed. I'd become completely absorbed in the drawing and felt calm and relaxed as I left for home.''

Losing yourself in a project can be an excellent problem-solving technique. Frequently, if you've been analyzing or weighing a problem and trying to come up with a solution, an answer will often pop into your conscious mind when you are ''lost'' in a project.

Building our self-esteem is a process. Though we'd all like to make changes that would build our self-esteem instantly, it just doesn't work that way. It's built piece by piece, day by day. And the good news is that one step forward frequently leads to another step forward, resulting in the start of a positive cycle. Here's another example of how this works.

Betty's Story
I . . . decided I'd get up a half hour earlier than usual.

Betty decided that she needed quiet time just for herself—away from husband, children, activities, and day-to-day responsibilities. She sat down one night to consider her options.

''I wanted twenty minutes a day for myself,'' Betty recalls. ''Evenings seemed impossible. Various activities, dinner, and time I wanted to spend with my husband seemed to keep me from finding twenty minutes just for myself unless I stayed up quite late, and I was definitely *not* a late-night person. My eyes tended to droop even before the end of the 10:00 P.M. news. I loved early morning, though, and decided I'd get up a half hour earlier than usual and try to create a peaceful start to the morning rather than the usual rush-and-tumble environment.

"I'd quietly get up at 6:00 A.M., walk to a part of the den that I'd set up as 'my space,' then turn on a relaxation tape and spend twenty to thirty minutes relaxing. I play tapes that provide relaxation exercises and guided imagery exercises. Then I listen to a tape that includes relaxation exercises followed by just music. I use this tape for relaxation and meditation. I've faithfully stuck with this schedule and have started noticing some changes. I feel less tense during the day and feel better able to cope with major and minor crises when they arise. During or following my meditation, I occasionally have insights or ideas about how to deal with a particular situation. It's difficult to say precisely what changes have occurred within me, but I do feel calmer and more confident—less likely to be thrown off center by anything that happens during the day."

The peacefulness Betty has found not only makes a difference in the quality of her life, but in her ability to take other steps forward. For instance, she began to realize that she really wanted to take two college business courses. She not only completed them, but finished her degree and started a part-time business.

Betty says that through her "found" moments of early morning relaxation and meditation, she was able to get in touch with parts of herself that she'd been forgetting. As she gained a better understanding of her needs and desires, she began to act on them. Though she initially felt some resistance from her family when she started her business courses, she talked to each of them about how crucial these courses were to her sense of self. Gradually they accepted the changes. Their initial skepticism changed to support and encouragement as they saw Betty feel better about herself. They realized that as she felt better about herself, they *also* gained. She was "there" for them— present to them in a positive, new way.

"As I became more attuned to myself, I also became more attuned to my body. I began walking more and began changing some of my family's meals to make them healthier."

These changes didn't happen overnight, but over a three-year period. It's been an evolution for Betty and her family, but an evolution that started with one small step—her wish to create some quiet time just for herself. Betty paid attention to important inner signals all along the way. As she acted on those inner urgings, she felt a sense of aliveness and joy in how she went about living her daily life that she'd not experienced before. She began to trust herself; she became proactive instead of reactive, taking responsibility for what she wished her life to be. As her sense of self grew, so did her confidence and her trust in the process. Not only did Betty's self-esteem grow, but she was better able to meet the needs of others in her life once she started meeting her own needs.

Being True to Ourselves

As discussed earlier, one of the things that keeps us from meeting our own needs is the tendency of many adult children to fall into the "people-pleasing" mode of behavior. In many instances we grew up trying to protect ourselves physically and emotionally. We learned many "survival" techniques. These may have been helpful when we were in an alcoholic or dysfunctional environment, but they may not be so useful to us now. Being authentic or true to ourselves is an important step in the development of our self-esteem and self-worth.

When we disagree with someone's statement, we may have a tendency to go along with it anyway so we don't create waves. We may not give our opinion if it differs from what a significant other or authority figure has said. We may force a laugh at something we do not really find amusing or act on a value we do not really believe in. Each time we act in such a way, we lose a piece of ourselves. Each time we cover up or submerge what our thoughts and feelings are, we chip away at our sense of self. We *can* learn to care for someone and yet still disagree. We *can* learn to say no without becoming paralyzed by fear or becoming worried about abandonment.

We've practiced habitual responses for many years as a way of seeking approval. Habits can be changed by practicing new behaviors. Each time we state our beliefs or say no when our tendency is to say yes, we are building a new habit. It will feel uncomfortable at first. Any change is uncomfortable. But don't let that feeling of discomfort deter you or plant doubts in your mind. It's natural to feel ill at ease when you're acting against a form of behavior that you've learned through years of practice. But with each *no* or each action that shows what you really feel and want, you will be one step further along the road of recovery. And with each *no*, you will be practicing a new behavior that will reaffirm your sense of self.

Quite literally, you may experience a real glow and surge of energy and confidence when you act with authenticity. Let's look at some examples of how this works.

Jean and Sharon's Story
Getting the Message Across

Jean's best friend, Sharon, was a highly successful businesswoman who did things quickly; Sharon's mind worked quickly, and she completed work very quickly. Sharon believed that one of the reasons for her success was her ability to be extremely efficient. She prided herself on accomplishing more than one thing at a time. If she was with someone who spoke very slowly and moved slowly, she'd find herself irritated. Jean became aware that when she and Sharon were on the phone talking, Sharon would be doing something else at the same time—opening mail or paying bills, for instance.

Jean realized that this was bothering her. She felt hurt that her friend didn't seem to care enough about her to pay full attention to what she was saying. Somehow, the process felt disrespectful to her. After one particular conversation, Jean felt especially upset because she sensed that Sharon's attention had been far more absorbed by her other task than by what she was saying. Jean thought about her reaction for a while and realized that she needed to share her feelings with Sharon. This was a very hard decision. Sharon and Jean were best friends and neither of them liked confrontation. Jean worried that this conversation could hurt or destroy their friendship.

When Jean finally worked up the courage to talk with Sharon, Sharon was very surprised and a little irritated to learn of Jean's feelings. Still, Jean felt very positive after the conversation. She had let her feelings be known and had expressed herself in a way that was calm and respectful but also conveyed her feelings. Although Sharon hasn't totally given up this habit of doing two things at once, Jean feels far better for having stated her thoughts openly and clearly.

Rick and Leslie's Story
Speaking One's Mind Has Positive Results

Rick and Leslie had been seeing each other for five months and had decided to make their relationship exclusive. For the past two weekends, they had spent time with other couples, and although Leslie had enjoyed these get-togethers, she became aware that she really missed having "alone" time with Rick. The following week when they were discussing their plans for the upcoming weekend, Leslie decided to be very direct and let Rick know her feelings. She said she had enjoyed the last two weekends, but she needed time over the weekend to be with just him. Although Leslie felt uncomfortable letting her feelings be known, she felt safe enough in the relationship to take a chance. She sensed Rick felt good that she wanted time with just him, and they decided they'd plan a way to make sure this would happen for them. They both ended up feeling very good about the process and how direct and honest they were with each other.

Karen and Ed's Story
Honesty Also Has Positive Results

Karen and Ed had been seeing each other for eight months and were not dating other people. One evening Ed talked about his ex-wife. Like Karen, Ed's ex-wife had come from an alcoholic home, but she had never learned how to deal effectively with her anger. Karen and Ed talked about specific examples of his ex-wife's anger and its impact on Karen and Ed's relationship. Karen knew that Ed had spent time in group sessions and had done a lot of reading to understand and deal with the problem.

She asked if he had ever seen the adult children's sheet that defines "the problem" and "the solution." Since he hadn't, she dug through a file and found it for him. As he was reading through the list of problems, she felt fear and shame well up in her stomach. She thought, *My God, when he looks at that list and reads all those problems, he'll probably walk out that door. Why would he want anything to do with me?*

About ten minutes later, she decided she had to talk about those feelings. As they sat on the couch in the living room, she told Ed that she felt scared and anxious as he read over that list. He indicated that he knew her well enough to know who she was as a person. He also realized from several previous conversations with Karen that there were several issues on the list that she was dealing with. But he recognized she was aware of these issues and admired her for confronting them and dealing with them head on. Tears of relief and happiness slid down her cheeks as she gave him a hug.

As you develop your ability to feel your feelings, accept your feelings, and talk about your feelings with those you trust, you will feel clearer and stronger. You will feel surges of confidence and energy that will serve as a reinforcement for each step forward that you take in this process. Gradually, step by step, you will build new, healthy behaviors that will provide rewards for you *and* for those you love. Gradually, step by step, you will be building your sense of self-esteem. It's a lifelong process, but you've already started the journey. And the journey will continue to reward you each step along the way.

CHAPTER SIX

||||||||||||||||||||||||||||||||||||||||||||||||||||||||||||||||||||||||||||||||||||

Taking Responsibility
For Ourselves—Putting
Ourselves First

In creating a successful recovery program for ourselves, most of us recognize that we have to take responsibility for our lives. The old excuses of blaming our parents, acting like victims, or playing martyrs wear thin with time. We may have set them aside and looked for new ways of acting and growing. But many of us—especially those of us adult children who learned and developed a ''caretaker'' personality—have a difficult time taking care of our needs first. Asking the question, *What do I want?* frequently feels foreign. And for those of us who are women, this task is especially difficult since our culture and our upbringing train us to be nurturers.

But, very often, when we take care of our needs first, we are much better able to be with others in a way that is positive for them and for us. No longer are we consciously or unconsciously storing resentment, anger, or frustration at not having our needs met, so we can approach situations and the important people in our lives with honesty, directness, and creativity. We take responsibility for ourselves. Some examples follow on how this works.

Nick's Story

We relaxed in the sun, barbecued hamburgers, and hiked along a favorite trail.

As Nick talked, there was pain in his voice. He and his wife had not been able to solve several conflicts. They kept going over the same ground again and again with no successful resolution. The frustration in his voice was heavy. He mentioned, though, that something unusual had occurred the previous weekend. Nick is an avid outdoor enthusiast, and between responsibilities for a home and a full-time job, he hadn't found time in recent months to get out to a park or walk a nature trail. Suddenly, he'd exclaimed to his family, "It's a beautiful day. Let's pack a picnic and go out to the park."

Nick recalls what happened. "We relaxed in the sun, barbecued hamburgers, and hiked along a favorite trail. As the smell of the woods, the moss, the trees, the wildflowers, and the water filled my head, I heard myself offering an option to my wife for solving one of the problems we'd been unable to resolve. Not only was the option new, but my approach in communicating this option was also new.

"I found myself somewhat startled, pleased, and amazed," he recalls, "when my wife responded positively rather than defensively. The whole feel and approach to the problem resolution were different and it worked."

Perhaps without even consciously realizing what he was doing, Nick was taking care of his own needs when he suggested that the family head off on a picnic. Being in a favorite setting created a sense of relaxation and peacefulness: frequently, this can be conducive to creativity and problem solving. Without even consciously processing the idea, Nick had found a new approach, and he was able to present it in a manner that was not defensive or blaming. And his wife responded favorably.

Tina's Story

. . . our physician also told me that Frank had cancer in the lungs.

Tina also recently took care of herself but, unlike Nick, she was very conscious of the choices she was creating. What she hadn't expected were the many benefits she hadn't even anticipated that she gained from this process.

"My husband, Frank, and I had been on a roller coaster of

hope, tension, and worry during the last eight months. Frank was diagnosed with a lung condition called *fibrosis*. Tests, exploratory surgery, cortisone treatment, and worry over the progression of the disease created tension. At one point our physician told me that Frank also had cancer in the lungs. But after more tests, he reversed this diagnosis. But after consulting a second specialist and many more tests, the cancer diagnosis was confirmed.

"Shortly afterward, Frank learned of a family reunion planned for Washington state in several weeks and asked me if we could drive out together. I carefully considered this request, and with some guilt said no, I would not attend, but I felt it would be wonderful for Frank to go on his own."

Tina's "no" resulted from a very careful consideration of her own needs as well as Frank's. She was tense, tired, and felt very worried about Frank's illness. She realized that she needed a break from the constant worry, and spending time alone and with friends over the two weeks Frank would be gone would give her perspective. Staying home would provide needed time for activities she enjoyed that didn't interest Frank. Since she had been so involved with Frank and his illness, many of these interests and activities had been dropped during the past eight months.

"A friend and I went out to dinner and a movie one night. When we talked on the phone later in the week, just before Frank was expected home, my friend had started to laugh. She noted there wasn't one night in the past two weeks when I had been at home. She said I sounded relaxed, happy, and rejuvenated. My friend wondered if the tension and worry would return to my voice when Frank returned from the reunion.

"My friend talked to me again several days after Frank's return. She pointed out that my voice remained calm and relaxed as I related what a wonderful time Frank had had in Washington."

Tina also said that the two weeks on her own had done something else for her that she'd not consciously anticipated. Before Frank left on the trip, Tina felt a great deal of fear about being alone should Frank not recover. She now explained that during those two weeks on her own she'd learned she *could survive* being alone if Frank died. She knew it would be hard, but she'd experienced the love of friends and enjoyable activities during the past two weeks. She knew that should Frank not make it, she was strong and capable and could make a good life for herself. There was confidence and strength in her voice.

She also realized that she tried very hard to get Frank to take an active role with his illness. She had suggested tapes, books, and courses about coping with his disease. She now decided that she would make one last comment about the availability of such resources but would then let it drop. Frank had to take responsibility for himself. She couldn't and wouldn't do it for him.

"The decision *not* to accompany Frank to his reunion was very difficult for me," Tina says now. "Many friends and co-workers expressed surprise and sometimes outright disapproval that I was not accompanying my husband—especially in light of his illness."

But Tina knew herself and her needs well. She spent two weeks gaining a better understanding of her strength, developing a broader perspective, and regaining her sense of self. And she came to an understanding of what she could and couldn't do for Frank. Tina's understanding is making their relationship more positive during a time of tension and turmoil for them both.

All of us involved in the recovery process might learn something of value from Tina's approach. Though she admits that at first she felt somewhat guilty about her decision not to accompany Frank to his reunion, she'd not made the decision impulsively. She'd taken good care of herself in the process. Tina had given herself ample time to make the decision, and she had used a variety of decision-making approaches:

- She'd very logically listed the pros and cons of attending the reunion.
- Then she'd given herself a break from thinking about the situation.
- Next, she'd asked for guidance in making the decision and

had specifically asked for such guidance prior to her morning meditation period.

The "inner voice" that responded to her question "felt right" to Tina, but she decided to ask for guidance a second time. When she received the same feeling a second time, she knew that she was getting guidance from the inner part of herself that she could trust. She paid attention to her inner guidance and never felt at any step along the way that she'd taken the wrong turn. In Chapter Twelve we'll talk more about "inner guidance" or intuition.

Trusting our inner voice and taking responsibility for ourselves are two crucial pieces in putting together the puzzle of our recovery process. When we decide to take care of ourselves, we are affirming our value as human beings worthy of unconditional caring and love. We are affirming that our hopes, dreams, and concerns are not only valid, but important. We are saying that what and who we are is important. When we are able to reach this point in our recovery, we will have the wind to our backs for smoother sailing, no matter how choppy the seas ahead may become.

CHAPTER SEVEN

||||||||||||||||||||||||||||||||||||||||||||||||||||||||||||||||||||||

Coping with High Expectations

There is a paradox for us as adult children in learning about our purpose in life and then setting goals to support that purpose. For a while, it may seem as if we are doing very well with this process. Our life may begin to smooth out; we may find ourselves moving closer and closer to our dreams. In fact, we may actually realize some of our dreams quickly once we learn to use our energies to our best advantage. But not surprisingly, most of us as adult children have learned to not trust in outcomes and to expect too much of ourselves and our recovery programs. This can be a dangerous and potentially lethal combination that can keep us from reaching our dreams. But it's something we can overcome if we are aware of it.

Evelyn's Story
Gingerbread Houses

Last September a memory from childhood flashed into Evelyn's mind. It was her eighth birthday party. She sat at a table with six other little girls, and they were decorating gingerbread houses. The memory was vivid and joyful. Then and there she decided she'd invite her closest friends over to her house to decorate gingerbread houses for her forty-first birthday. The thought of being surrounded by her closest friends was the most powerful, positive feeling about this celebration, but the creative and artistic part of her also loved the idea of decorating

71

the gingerbread houses. She rarely expressed the artistic side of herself, and this definitely appealed to the "artist within."

One of her dearest friends, knowing of her excitement about the upcoming party, bought her a gingerbread mold for Christmas, so she was set. On her trips to the grocery store for several weeks prior to the party, she bought bottles of "sprinkles" and frosting in all colors to decorate the gingerbread houses. This gradual accumulation of supplies for the party was intentional—partly for reasons of cash flow—but more importantly, for building anticipation and prolonging the period of enjoyment.

The week before the party, Evelyn spent her evenings mixing dough and baking the fourteen molds for the gingerbread houses. She also decided that since her friends were coming over to help her celebrate on Sunday, she'd take a vacation day on Monday, her actual birthday. Since a good friend had raved about how wonderful it felt to get a facial, she also decided to treat herself to a facial and a massage on her day off. On the night of her birthday, the company she worked for just happened to be sponsoring a benefit performance by the Kingston Trio at a local theater. The Kingston Trio just happened to be a favorite group of hers from many years back. Evelyn invited the man she'd been dating to go with her. All in all, she was looking forward to two days of really wonderful celebration.

"The image that I continued to carry around in my head was one of being surrounded by the love and joy of my friends as we made gingerbread houses," she recalls. "The image was so vivid and powerful for me because the year before my best friend had thrown a surprise party for my fortieth birthday. Walking into that room full of my friends on my birthday was one of the most beautiful experiences of my life. The feeling of love and joy and support was overwhelming. Since many of my friends didn't know each other, it was wonderful to have them meet. Often during the next year when I was somewhat down about an experience or event, I'd purposely conjure up the image of walking into that room full of friends and let myself feel the love and support once again. It remains a very vivid and intense image for me."

On the day of Evelyn's forty-first birthday party, after several friends had already arrived, she received a call from two of her friends saying they couldn't make it. Although the five who did make gingerbread houses had a really fun afternoon, Evelyn felt disappointed that her vision of being surrounded by all her good friends hadn't come to pass. It somewhat clouded her full enjoyment of the party, even though her guests had a good time.

She realized she had created a very high expectation for this party and had, in effect, set herself up for disappointment.

"On my day off the following day, I had planned the morning so that I could get laundry and ironing done and then really relax the rest of the day with the facial and massage. About five minutes after I completed the housework, I received a call from my best childhood friend. Then, in quick succession, I received calls from my sister, my father, and another of my good friends. In contrast to the day before when I had tremendously high expectations and a vivid image of exactly how I wanted things to go, I'd not really had any strong expectations for that Monday morning and had been very pleasantly surprised by the phone calls."

Evelyn's birthday experience is a vivid reminder of a pattern that is quite typical for many people who grew up in alcoholic homes: *the high expectation syndrome*. We seem to have an extraordinary ability to expect perfection in ourselves or events, and when things don't go exactly as planned or imagined, we find it equally as easy to descend in a spiral of disappointment and regret. Many times these feelings can also trigger despair, emptiness, and hopelessness as we chastise ourselves once again for the "stupidity" of our actions. The old saying, "The higher they go, the harder they fall" seems apt. Some say our tendency to set high expectations is a result of our *need* to fail. Failures deserve to be punished, and so we punish ourselves. We just about guarantee such an outcome when we set our sights at the highest possible point.

Several other aspects of this high expectation cycle are also important to look at. For instance, no matter *what* we do, it's usually not good enough. Or when we get close to accomplishing our goals, we change the rules. Or we *do* achieve the goal, and then we minimize our achievement. When we think we have failed, our frustration, anger, depression, and loneliness can lead to compulsive behavior related to shopping, working, sleeping, drinking, or eating that can keep us from being in touch with our feelings. We need to change back to rules that are reasonable and supportive so we can effectively cope with our natural tendency toward high expectations.

CHAPTER EIGHT

||||||||||||||||||||||||||||||||||||||||||||||||||||||||||||||||||||||||||||

Handling "Slippery" Situations

Along with high expectations, it is not unusual for us to put ourselves in events or activities where old behaviors can surface: *slippery situations* we call them. Along with expecting too much of certain activities, we can set ourselves up for a fall by being with people who still practice behaviors that we're attempting to dislodge from our lives. We don't think ahead to possible outcomes that may threaten our serenity and well-being. Ginger's story is an example of such an occurrence.

Ginger's Story
I started putting together a plan of positive action.

When Ginger returned home to Minneapolis after visiting her sister in Chicago two and one-half years ago, she was depressed and angry with herself. For some reason that she couldn't pinpoint, she'd fallen back into old, negative eating and thinking patterns.

"A year earlier I had cut out sugar from my diet due to the negative effects it had on me," Ginger remembers. "An hour after eating cookies, candy, muffins, or just about any food with a heavy sugar content, I'd get very tired. The following day I'd have a splitting headache, feel crabby, and would not be able to concentrate well. My pattern of years of compulsive sweet eating had, I thought, come to a halt. But while visiting my sister, I compulsively ate cookies and didn't exercise at all.

I gained five pounds and slipped back into crabbiness, depression, and passivity. I knew better, yet there I was again.

"I vowed after that experience that on the next visit, I wouldn't let my old, negative pattern resurface. I wouldn't let myself eat even one cookie—because one cookie would set off a sweet eating binge.

"On the next visit, I *did* do better. No sweets. But I still sometimes slipped into old feelings of helplessness and passivity. I'd eliminated a negative pattern, but realized that I hadn't really substituted any positive pattern in its place. I knew that on my next trip to Chicago I needed a full-blown, positive plan of action. Perhaps others might have realized the need for such an approach earlier, but I was a little slow to figure out how to handle 'slippery situations.' "

Ginger learned of a seminar in Chicago she wished to attend. Since it was scheduled the Monday and Tuesday before Christmas, she decided it would be fun to spend the entire week before Christmas with her sister—especially since her niece, Dee, and her husband, Jorge, and their fifteen-month-old baby, Nicholas, would also be at her sister's. Since Dee and her family had been living in Mexico, Ginger had never met Jorge or seen Nicholas. Ginger was really looking forward to the visit.

"As soon as I finalized plans for the conference and with my sister, I started putting together a plan of positive action. I would take some of the foods I regularly ate with me since my sister usually ate meals heavy in fat and meat. I would make sure my diet stayed on track by taking along mineral water, fruits, vegetables, and homemade oat bread. In addition, I asked my sister if she would check to see if there were aerobics classes that I could take. I knew I would need to get some exercise to keep from feeling sluggish. I also made plans to visit my best friend, have lunch with an acquaintance who had just moved to Chicago, and spend a day at the Art Institute of Chicago. Since I was not fond of driving long distances by myself, I made plans to make the drive to Chicago as painless as possible. I decided to take my boom box and supply of tapes, because I enjoyed music and in several long stretches of Wisconsin, my car radio received only static. I even bought new tapes so I'd have the added advantage of looking forward to listening to new music."

Though Ginger didn't stick to the "Chicago Plan" precisely—she never did make it to the art institute or aerobics classes—it worked. Instead of aerobics, she took long walks each day around a lake. That was an unexpected bonus since she loved being around the serenity of woods and lakes. Those lake walks also helped her map a strategy for a problem she'd been wrestling with for several days. The time spent at the seminar and with her best friend from school days was extremely energizing.

What can be learned from these experiences? One of the main things Ginger learned is that she must take the responsibility to meet her own needs and create her own happiness. She knows that passivity, inactivity, poor diet, and lack of exercise trigger old thought patterns and actions that are not part of her recovery program and that send her spiraling back to negative experiences. When she thinks about her needs and takes action to meet them, she not only keeps her self-esteem healthy, but she also becomes much more fun, interesting, and loving to those around her.

Planning Ahead to Short-Circuit the Old System

Being around one's family, going to old "haunts," and participating in certain activities from prerecovery days can be a slippery business for all adult children. In these situations, it's natural for old feelings and thought patterns to surface. But learning to be proactive and planning ahead can short-circuit the old systems. Decide ahead of time what activities and experiences would feel good for you and add to your sense of well-being and happiness. Then map out a plan of action and carry out those activities. This will probably result in a positive outcome.

Perhaps this sounds like a lot of work, but the planning can become a pleasant and creative challenge. Consciously sitting down and brainstorming activities can not only make you feel good but can also build a sense of anticipation and accomplishment. Just realizing that you are taking responsibility for having a good time and allowing yourself to really experience that sense of good time as you plan your activities will create a positive flow of feelings. Visualizing yourself enjoying the activities you've planned can also firmly implant the positive feelings in your subconscious. This further ensures that you will carry through with your plan of action.

Remaining somewhat flexible and accepting the fact that you may not carry out your plan perfectly is also important. Ginger could have berated herself for not getting to aerobics classes or to the art institute when she visited her sister in Chicago. Instead, she went with the flow of activities and appreciated the shifts along the way that led to even more positive experiences. One such shift was walking around the nearby lake. This provided peaceful moments and a calming influence that may not have been part of the experience in an aerobics class. Spending an evening in the emergency room of a hospital with her best friend from Chicago was not what either of them had planned, but it was an experience that reemphasized the closeness they shared. They laughed about the experience, because the last time Ginger's best friend had visited Minneapolis, she had spent the evening in the emergency room with Ginger as Ginger had seven stitches put in her forehead! They decided enough was enough. Since they'd now each had their emergency room experience, it was time to move on to other experiences together!

Developing a plan of action for "slippery" places, people, or events and carrying through on the plan can be truly exhilarating. It can provide positive reinforcement as you continue in recovery. Write down your success and tack it on your bulletin board or tape it on your mirror as a positive reminder of the progress you are making. You can't remind yourself too often of your victories—no matter how large or small those victories are.

CHAPTER NINE

▌▌

Cultivating a Sense of Commitment

A scientist watched a monarch butterfly struggling to emerge from its cocoon. The creature pulled and pushed, tearing at the rough material of the cocoon. The scientist, watching this lengthy battle, thought that if he snipped the last bit of cocoon with his scissors, he could help this struggling creature. But when he cut away the last piece of the cocoon, the butterfly seemed to grow weaker and, finally, with its wings still partly folded, it fell back on the table—dead. As the butterfly emerged from the cocoon, each push against the cocoon forced lifeblood into its wings. And the butterfly would have been only able to fly once it had completed this process. The scientist realized that by trying to make things easier, he had actually killed the butterfly.

If the path to recovery seems to be an obstacle course instead of a fairly well-marked path, just remember the story of the butterfly. With each effort and each struggle, we push further away from the "cocoon." With each healthy decision, we come closer to being like the creature whose wings are breathtakingly beautiful and whose flight is effortless.

Nowhere is it written that there won't continue to be struggles, disappointments, and valleys. That's just the way it is, and we have no control over many of life's situations. But we do have control over how we *react* to and handle those situations. Take the case of Hal.

Hal's Story
I had no control over the ultimate decision. . . .

Hal had been working hard at his job over the past three
years. But during this time he had also made known his interest
in developing and expanding a department in his company. In
the last six months, the timing had improved for expanding the
department, and he'd spent much time and energy (including
vacation time) preparing reports, researching information, and
preparing budget estimates. He'd received signals that the project could move forward, and the company had even sent him
to Washington, D.C., to talk with several key contacts.

"Though I'd tried to be realistic and keep my expectations
down, during the last two weeks my hopes had been buoyed.
The president of the company sent me a copy of a letter he'd
written that indicated I'd be managing this new department.
But by the end of the same week, it was apparent that the
expansion of the department was still very much in limbo. A
Friday meeting had been discouraging. The budget figures
looked too risky. I had started to see myself in this new position. If it wasn't going to happen, what would I do? I'd been
thinking about this opportunity and had persisted with conversations and ideas related to the project for three years. There
were really no other opportunities for advancement at my company. What would I do?

"I was extremely disappointed and discouraged and spent a
full twenty-four-hour period in a depressed state. After this
initial period of disappointment, I realized it was necessary for
me to detach from the situation. I had no control over the
ultimate decision of whether the company would move ahead
on the project. I could only do my best in gathering and presenting information. Gradually, over the next few days, I was
able to look at the situation and see some amusement in it.
With this detachment came the ability to step back and ask
myself, *Well, now what? If this goal doesn't come to fruition,
then what do I do?*"

The week before Hal's project was in a state of limbo, Hal
and a colleague had been invited to present a workshop to high

school honor students. He loved doing it. He began to realize that he could use the energy he had gained from this experience and work toward a new goal—presenting workshops on a topic he loved to students and other groups. He decided to do it on a part-time basis initially and build on that for the future. Who knew where it might eventually lead? And in the meantime, he'd really enjoy doing it. He'd also take a fresh look at his current job and find new ways to make it more challenging, so he could get more enjoyment out of it.

Commitment to any kind of goal is not always easy, and the outcome may not always be what we might initially wish. But commitment brings a sense of direction and energy to our lives. In Hal's case, there were certainly gains along the way as he focused his energy and enthusiasm into the project. He learned a great deal about areas of company operation he'd not been familiar with previously. His reports had been well researched and written, so he'd gained new respect in the eyes of his superiors. And most importantly, he was able to detach from the outcome after his initial disappointment, and he was able to decide on a new avenue where he could channel his ability and enthusiasm if the project at his company didn't come through.

Commitment does demand focused energy as well as time directed toward a particular goal. We adult children will probably not need much practice in focusing on a particular outcome. But we may need to practice enjoying the process along the way, maintaining an attitude of hope, and focusing on positive options when outcomes aren't what we wish.

Let's take an example of being committed to a relationship with a spouse or significant other. We are enjoying the relationship and are committed to our own happiness as well as to our partner's. But let's say a few minor irritations surface. Let's say our partner is very often late. A first reaction might be irritation and anger. But before reacting, consider the options. That's what Teresa did.

Teresa's Story

After sitting down and creating choices for herself, Teresa felt much better.

Teresa remembers sitting down and consciously analyzing the situation. *There are four ways I can think of to deal with it: (1) I can just accept the fact that Bill is frequently late and not get upset about it; (2) I can tell him to come one-half hour earlier than he really needs to in order to build some leeway; (3) when it is a special event or outing with friends, I can indicate that it is very important to be on time and would appreciate his help; (4) I can ask him to participate in the process of determining solutions or ideas so the habit can be discussed very openly and directly.*

After sitting down and creating these choices for herself, Teresa felt much better. She didn't let her initial irritation cause her to react in a way that would have had a predictable—and negative—outcome. Several of her choices proved to be very effective.

The paradox of commitment is that it is the greatest freedom of all. Once we focus on our commitment, we are free to direct our energy—our physical, spiritual, and mental resources—toward a goal about which we feel very passionate. And that is important, since the key to commitment is to determine what you love and include more of what you love in your life.

CHAPTER TEN

||||||||||||||||||||||||||||||||||||||||||||||||||||||||||||||||||||||||||||||||||

Designing Your Reward System

Think a moment about your favorite activities. Do you like to swim? Putter around with wood or clay? Maybe you are a railroad enthusiast and like to play with miniature train sets. Perhaps reading magazines is high on your list or watching old movies on television on Saturday afternoon. Whatever the activities are, just relax a moment and think about what you enjoy doing.

So often we don't give ourselves permission to take the time to do the things we really love. Many times we feel too pressured or too overwhelmed by day-to-day responsibilities. But, ironically, if we'd let ourselves take the time for hobbies, projects, or other pleasurable activities, we'd find that we would be much more effective at dealing with items on our "to do" list.

By giving ourselves rewards for steps forward along the way in our recovery process or for other accomplishments, we are reinforcing the behavior we want to incorporate into our lives. Learning theory tells us that such reinforcement is important in learning. It also tells us that the more ways we choose to reinforce the behavior, the more likely we'll repeat the behavior. For instance, if you have recently spoken up for yourself in a situation where you might have previously buried your feelings, you could choose several different ways to reinforce this behavior. You could write out the experience in your journal or on a note pad. Living through the experience again as you write about it reinforces the experience in your mind. Or you might choose to relax, close your eyes, and visualize the experience once again in your mind. Another option would be to call a trusted friend and let him or her know about your accomplishment so that you, once again, can relive it.

Jenny's Story
Being Straightforward and Honest

Recently Jenny took a risk. She told the man she'd been dating about some of her feelings of sadness after a family visit. As she talked about her feelings and cried, he held her in his arms. When she stopped talking, he said: "I'm really glad you told me about these things. It gives me a much better understanding of some of the things that were hard for you as a young girl." She felt as if a huge weight had been removed from her shoulders after sharing this information. Not only that, but she and Ted felt an even closer bond. A few days after sharing this experience with a close friend, the friend said, "Jenny, do you realize how far you've come? Being able to talk about those feelings with someone you deeply care about is wonderful. Not only that, but when you shared your feelings, you did it in a very straightforward way that was honest. Give yourself some credit for how much you've grown and changed."

Jenny relates what happened next. "About a week later, Ted called me early one morning to share his feelings and concerns about what he perceived had been happening between us over the last several days. We spent a half hour talking out the concerns, and both of us felt better after the conversation. In fact, I felt delighted when Ted called my office later that morning and happened to remark that as he'd driven himself to work that morning, he'd given himself a pat on the back for how he'd handled the situation. I was pleased he'd given himself credit for his communication skills. Several days later, I told him how glad I was that he'd congratulated himself for how he'd handled the situation."

Fred's Story

I had to "go through it to get around it."

Fred had recently decided to attend an Al-Anon meeting on Friday nights. One evening Fred invited a man in the group to his house after the meeting, so he could loan the man tapes Fred thought were useful. This man was trying to decide whether to stay with an alcoholic wife, a similar situation to one Fred had experienced fifteen years before. Fred had faced some difficult things that same evening in the group. He shared his feelings of sadness about his children. He and his children were estranged, and Fred felt particularly sad as Father's Day approached.

"Though the sadness and pain were difficult, I had to 'go through it to get around it,' " Fred said later. "I realized after I'd expressed my feelings of sadness and regret to my group that I'd really gotten through this time better than in previous years. I'd been able to bounce back faster and detach more quickly. I *did* commend myself for that and decided to share more of my experiences and progress with my group. I admitted that I was doing it as much for myself as for the other group members who might benefit from hearing about my experiences."

Besides writing down an account of your progress or sharing it with a friend, you may want to take your reward system one step further and plan something special for yourself. Sometimes the most commonplace things can satisfy your need for reward. Maybe a half hour reading the sports section will satisfy you or an hour of window shopping. Decide what rewards are reasonable, then strive to attain them.

Sarah's Story

By creating a reward system, I actually set a goal.

Sarah didn't have much extra money in her budget, but she loved flowers. She was working very hard at a full-time job and a part-time job, as well as raising a daughter and returning to school. Summers weren't a problem with her reward system since each spring she bought seeds and grew flowers in containers on her apartment deck. But winters were a problem.

"Several days after sharing with one of my friends my desire for weekly flowers, I was driving over to my friend Barbara's house to take Barbara to the airport," Sarah recalls. "I planned to go to my favorite park afterward. It was a beautiful, sunny spring day. I'd brought a book that I needed to finish for a class. If I had to work this weekend, I thought, at least I could sit outside and feel the breeze and the sun as I read. I also thought that there might be some lilac bushes or other flowering bushes in the park so I might be able to gather some branches to take into the office the next day. It would be my first step in implementing my 'flower reward' system."

Sarah felt a sense of contentment as she drove over to Barbara's house. She was looking forward to talking with Barbara. As she walked into Barbara's house, the first thing she noticed was a vase full of beautiful red carnations and baby's breath. The first words Barbara spoke were: "Sarah, would you like to take those flowers home with you since I'll be out of town this week?" Sarah was delighted. It flashed through her mind that she'd taken Barbara to the airport many times, but this was the first time Barbara had ever mentioned flowers. And it was just three days ago that Sarah had decided on having flowers in her life regularly, and she had shared that thought with only one friend (not Barbara). What a wonderful example of how *synchronicity* (a word that basically means trusting in the outcome) can give us peace. We'll discuss the concept of synchronicity further in Chapter Seventeen.

Sarah tells what happened next. "I then decided to approach my situation with several creative ideas. I told my friends and colleagues about my desire to have flowers in my life regularly. Several of my friends would occasionally bring me small bouquets, which I would take to my office and enjoy all week. Or I would buy a full bouquet, or if I couldn't afford that, just one flower. A friend told me about a farmer's market where I could buy inexpensive flowers.

"By creating this reward system, I actually set a goal. I creatively came up with a variety of ideas to reach my goal and asked for support from my friends. When I walked into my office each morning, the flowers I saw there automatically produced a smile on my face. It was a positive way to start each day and a tangible reminder to me that I'd accomplished many positive things in my life during the past week. My joy set a positive tone for my morning, and that carried over into my entire attitude toward my work.''

Sarah's reward system of flowers is an example of how being good to yourself is not being selfish, but is a way to create a positive lifestyle. It can have multiple benefits. Not only does Sarah reinforce her positive accomplishments by having flowers in her office, but she also reinforces her goal-setting abilities. She learns to accept gifts of flowers from her friends—since asking for help and support has always been difficult for Sarah, this is an important factor—and her friends feel good about helping her. She has also noticed that others in her office enjoy seeing flowers—so her gift to herself also brings joy to others. Seeing the flowers each morning has a powerful, positive impact on her feelings and attitude, which certainly also impacts the work she does. Sarah has taken responsibility for asking for what she wants, has done some problem solving along the way, and has been gentle and kind to herself. Ultimately she's been rewarded for her positive accomplishments.

Although flowers may not be the reward system you choose, jot down thoughts on what reward system would make sense for you. Then brainstorm on your own or with friends. Find a way to incorporate the reward system into your life. In the long run, you'll probably be a happier and more productive person.

PART TWO

The Process of
Creating Choices

CHAPTER ELEVEN

‖‖‖

How the Process Can Work for You

In the following pages, we will take a closer look at how the process of creating choices works. It's a process that involves conscious choice making as well as letting go. It develops slowly for most of us as we gain a sense of trust in ourselves, our recovery, and the spiritual dimension of our lives. Let's take a look at how the process worked for Karen.

Karen's Story
Focusing Energy Toward a Goal

Two years ago Karen wrote some thoughts on what she wanted in her life. Among the five or six things she noted was a "wider circle of close friends." At that point she had several good friends but only one friend with whom she was particularly close. They shared nearly everything with each other, but Karen felt as if she were too dependent on her friend. Since Karen had no family nearby, Karen's friends *were* her family. But she knew that things change. It made sense that she should not be so dependent on one person and she should strive to make new friends and increase her capacity for intimacy along the way.

Although she didn't have a specific plan of action to make new friends, she did realize it was important to broaden her friendships. It was something that she knew couldn't be "forced."

Now, two years later, Karen has four new friends, one of whom has become particularly dear and close. How did this come about? Karen believes it happened through consciously focusing energy on the fact that new and deep friendships were important to her and her recovery process. She also learned more about her needs, who she was, and what she wanted in her life. This process of exploration led her to three of the four friendships.

"First, I met Carol," Karen recalls. "I had enjoyed several seminars at a church I'd attended occasionally. I decided to attend a weekend seminar offered on exploring a person's 'in-look' or inner attitude. I sat next to a woman named Carol who was very open and friendly. During one of the breaks, we somehow got on the topic of investing. Carol had obviously done a lot of research and was very knowledgeable. Since my divorce, money had been a tough issue for me. I was working two jobs and really needed good advice on how to get started—even with a very small amount of money to invest. We decided to get together for lunch. Carol said she'd be happy to bring some background information for me.

"On the day we were to meet, I was swamped with work. I tried to reach Carol to cancel the lunch, but I was too late; Carol had already left. I reluctantly headed out the door—thinking about deadlines and projects I was feeling under pressure to complete that afternoon. Over lunch, we managed to veer off into topics other than investing and got to know each other better.

"Over the next six months, our lunches became more regular. We were both working hard to make progress in recovery and shared many similar thoughts and feelings. Carol also was very logical and analytical, and I appreciated her insights. We shared ideas and books and built a solid friendship along the way."

Next, Karen met Alice. Alice and Karen were the only two people who signed up for a summer evening class in massage therapy. Alice taught English at a small, private school. Since Karen was teaching English part time, they had much to share. Not too many people other than English teachers could get excited about discussing short story analysis or methods of teaching grammar and writing!

"Melinda came into my life next," Karen says. "I was intrigued when I received a notice about the one-night-a-week, four-week class Melinda was teaching on 'inventuring' [based on the Richard Leider and Janet Hagberg book, *The Inventurers: Excursions in Life and Career Renewal*]. The group of over thirty people who signed up for the class was bright and interesting. Though I had read the book a number of years before, I sensed that sharing some of the processes outlined in the book with this group could be valuable. The students worked in small groups, and gradually we came to know and enjoy each other.

"For several months after the class ended, my small group continued to meet informally with Melinda. I was extremely impressed with Melinda's sensitivity, positive outlook, enthusiasm, and gift of caring. When Melinda called to invite me to lunch, I was flattered and pleased. Melinda and I decided to try and get together at least every other month. Melinda's a positive, wonderful blessing in my life and someone with whom I look forward to sharing many moments at a really 'gut' level."

The odds against Karen meeting Colleen the way she did must have been astronomical. Karen and Colleen had been sorority sisters at Miami University in Oxford, Ohio, and had last seen each other when they graduated in 1970. Karen was at the public television station where she worked on a Saturday night in March, helping out on one of the station's membership drives. She had done some on-air "pitching" to request memberships. As she walked out of the studio that night, the station's membership manager handed her a note to call Colleen. Karen was amazed and stunned. Colleen had been her favorite sorority sister, and Karen hadn't seen her or talked to her in twenty years. When Karen heard Colleen's voice on the phone, she felt like she'd been transported back twenty years. They made arrangements to get together for Sunday brunch.

"We both admitted later we were a little nervous about getting together," Karen says. "What if we had very little in common or nothing to say to each other? That worry disappeared the moment we sat down together. We talked nonstop for two and one-half hours. It was as if we'd never been apart.''

Karen did get what she asked for—the blessing of new friends in her life. But she certainly would never have anticipated or guessed that these new friends would enter her life in the way they did.

"Things Will Happen When They're Supposed to Happen"

Being *aware* of what you want in your life and focusing energy and concentration on that goal often brings amazing results. The results may not always come about in the way you might expect, but they do come about. That's why the old saying, ''Be careful what you ask for, you might get it'' is not something to be casually tossed aside. Indeed, you may *well* get what you ask for!

In addition to not always knowing *how* what you ask for may come into your life, it's not always possible to know *when*. For impatient types, this can be a real kicker. Wanting what you want and wanting it now is a fairly typical mind-set for those of us on a recovery path. That's where learning to trust and ''letting go'' become crucial. Learning to trust and letting go of your desire to control the outcome are two of the toughest things you may ever do.

So how *do* you do it? That's what we propose to discuss in detail in upcoming chapters. For the time being, you should realize that setting aside time just for you for relaxation exercises, meditation, hobbies, and affirmations may be one of the most important decisions you make in your recovery process. Feeling that you're worth this investment of time and acting on that feeling will help you spiritually and emotionally. You are making a decision to be the very best *you* possible. As Leo Buscaglia, the noted lecturer and author on human relations, once remarked, ''You can be the most wonderful, juicy, delicious plum in the world, but some people just don't like plums.

But if you try and change yourself into a banana, you'll always be a second-rate banana!''

Invest time in yourself to become the best you can be physically, emotionally, intellectually, and spiritually. As you grow and develop your potential in these areas, you'll attract many new activities, adventures, and friends. A powerful and positive snowball effect is created. As you make one change in your life that nurtures and aligns your "outer being" with your "inner, spiritual being," you will move closer to another positive change, and to another. It will happen when it's right for it to happen— which may not be on the same time line that you might want.

One technique you may want to try is filling out a "Six-Month Want List." Try writing down the things you would like to have in your life in the next six months. They can be small or large items—anything from a new shaver to a new career. It's especially helpful to share this process with a trusted friend.

Joe's Story
. . . he wouldn't have been ready for the realization of these goals in his life two years ago.

Joe joined a friend and, together, they wrote out their Six-Month Want Lists. Of the eight major goals Joe wrote, two were reached during the six-month period. Three other goals looked quite possible to reach within nine months. Two other goals were ongoing goals that Joe continues to work on regularly, and the last goal was one that really is no longer important to him. His desire would have been to have realized all these goals two years earlier. But now Joe realizes that in a number of important ways, he wouldn't have been ready for the realization of these goals in his life two years ago.

Although it's easy for Joe to see *now* that he wouldn't have been ready to handle the realization of these goals earlier in his life, he certainly *wouldn't* have realized this earlier. We must trust that things will happen when they're supposed to happen—when we are best able to deal with them. Remember the saying: "When the student is ready, the teacher appears."

CHAPTER TWELVE

██

Learning to Trust Your Intuition

Intuition is called "the sixth sense," "instinct," "an innate or inborn tendency," "the inner voice," or "a hunch." It is the experience of knowing who is on the phone before you pick it up; walking to the right counter in a large department store that you haven't been in before; taking a book off the shelf that proves to be interesting and valuable; or knowing when something is amiss with someone you love and finding out later that your "hunch" was correct.

Other words that are associated with intuition include *clairvoyance*, *presentiment*, *foreboding*, *suspicion*, and *apprehension*. All are used variously to describe the experience of knowing something before the event actually occurs or choosing to change course in the middle of an activity despite contrary facts or logic.

If you have ever said to yourself, *But I knew that all along*, trust yourself, you probably did! You intuitively knew the right answer. One of the goals of this book is to get you in touch with your inner voice so you can harness this incredible power and pursue your goals. This is not to suggest that learning to listen to your intuition will prevent you from making mistakes or failing at certain tasks. All of us fail, all of us make mistakes, all of us waste time and energy. But listening to that inner voice, that sense of right and wrong, can help you learn from mistakes and move from failure to success. If you listen to and honor your inner voice, you may achieve your goals more quickly. And you will feel very satisfied about honoring your wishes and ideas in the process.

You can contact your intuition and learn to actively seek guidance from it. Part of the process of developing trust in yourself and your recovery is learning how to trust your intuition. If you tend to be a people pleaser, trusting your feelings and reactions may be a new and somewhat uncomfortable experience. The three stories that follow will help illustrate how learning to trust your intuition can be extremely valuable to you—in many aspects of your life. Jenny's story is a classic example of harnessing the power of intuition.

Jenny's Story
I was startled and amazed by what had occurred.

"I woke up with a start at 3:30 A.M. I was wide awake," Jenny recalls. "Grabbing my journal and a pen from the wicker nightstand next to my bed, I began to write. After writing for twenty minutes and filling five pages of my journal, I paused, feeling amazed at the process that had just occurred. I had awakened with a full-blown understanding of the dynamics that were occurring with a man I'd been seeing. Such an experience had never happened to me, and I was startled and amazed by what had occurred. I knew at the deepest level of my being that the perceptions I'd recorded were true, yet how did I come to know this information?"

A week later over dinner at a restaurant that Jenny and Kurt both enjoyed, she shared with Kurt the early morning experience she'd recorded in her journal. She had never seen anyone literally turn white; the color completely drained from his face. When she finished recounting the details and went on to talk about something else, he said, "Go back to what you were talking about and tell me more." Jenny replied that she couldn't; there was no more. She could tell he was stunned. He didn't say a word, and he didn't have to. She knew from his reaction that the information she'd shared with him was accurate.

Since that experience three years ago, Jenny has had two

similar experiences. Although neither of these experiences felt as complete, or dramatic, or as full-blown as the first, they still offered valuable ideas and information. Because these experiences were valuable to Jenny, she has tried to purposefully induce similar experiences by concentrating on a situation she wants insight on before going to sleep. Although this process of seeking specific insight into a situation hasn't yet worked, she has read enough on dreaming to know that such a process can be successful, so she intends to keep trying.

There isn't a name or a label for what happened to Jenny. But many people have learned to value the information that comes to them through intuition. On the occasions when they've chosen to ignore their gut feelings, they've later deeply regretted the decision.

Doug's Story
What Can Happen When Intuition Is Ignored

Doug, an enthusiastic type, is somewhat impulsive at times. This is a quality he likes about himself but which he sometimes finds a need to temper. Frequently tuning in to his intuition can provide the direction he needs to determine if he should move forward with the "impulsive" idea.

But on one occasion Doug plunged right into a situation and ignored his intuition. "I had come across a description of a college course that seemed in tune with my philosophy. I thought it would be fun to share ideas and experiences with someone who held a similar philosophy. When I called the instructor, he seemed hesitant to get together, asked many questions, and seemed very suspicious. He reluctantly agreed to meet for lunch. Red flags of warning were popping up as I got off the phone. I seriously considered canceling the lunch, but I felt a little ridiculous for being so uneasy."

Doug chose to ignore these warnings. Not only was the lunch unpleasant, but he felt angry at himself for ignoring his intuitive feelings about the meeting. For several days, he kept saying to himself, *I knew better!* Needless to say, he learned a valuable lesson.

Leah's Story

Of course I felt comfortable! I was back in an alcoholic environment again.

After Leah's divorce, she met a man she was attracted to, but some discomfort and uneasiness settled in during the second date. She had gone with her date, her roommate, and her roommate's fiancé to a restaurant for lunch that was famous city-wide for mouth-watering roast beef sandwiches. Her roommate's fiancé and Leah's date seemed to get along well and drank beer after beer, proceeding to get quite drunk. "Coming from an alcoholic home," Leah recalls, "I felt some discomfort, but chose to ignore the incident.

"On a subsequent date, I wanted to tell this man why I didn't drink. As I shared the story of my mother's alcoholism with Jerry, he, ironically, sat drinking a beer. Afterward, he told me, with obvious pain in his voice, about his second wife walking out on him. But Jerry spent most of the time telling me that what upset him so much about the incident was that she took his case of chilled beer out of the refrigerator and left it in the middle of the kitchen floor to get warm."

When Leah finally stopped denying consciously what her subconscious mind knew all along—that this man was an alcoholic—she realized why she had been so comfortable with Jerry for close to a year. "Of course I felt comfortable! I was back in an alcoholic environment again."

Never talking about what she wanted, expected, or what was happening in the relationship was the accepted pattern, and that *did* feel normal to Leah. When things began to get rocky in the last three months of the relationship, she felt great fear, which made her cling more tightly to the relationship. When it ended, Leah was devastated.

"Though I was deeply depressed for several months, I started reading and attending workshops for adult children of alcoholics. The breakup was painful. But it forced me to take a good, long, hard look at my life. I later found myself thanking Jerry. Without the pain and devastation, I might not have started on the road to recovery."

Trusting our instincts, radar, intuition—whatever terms we wish to use—is an important part of many recovering people's lives. And even though we may tend to be enthusiastic, impulsive types, many of us have learned to give ourselves a little space and time to listen to our inner voice. By meditating or practicing relaxation exercises, we can calm the chattering box inside our heads long enough to let the still, calm voice of "knowing" come to the forefront of conscious understanding. Our inner voice is there for each of us and can be a powerful tool in our recovery process.

Trusting our intuition nurtures the process of learning to trust and love, which are important steps in our recovery process. First and foremost, we need to trust that we will be there to nurture and care for ourselves, that we will pay attention to our own wants and needs, and that we will act on those wants and needs.

CHAPTER THIRTEEN

||||||||||||||||||||||||||||||||||||||||||||||||||||||||||||||||||||||||||

Mindfulness: Creating
An Attitude of Joy

Conscious choice making is part of the skill involved in living life "mindfully." As sixteenth president of the United States Abraham Lincoln once said, "A human being is about as happy as he makes up his mind to be." There is a great deal of truth in that statement.

In Southeast Asia, a clever trap is used to catch monkeys. Hunters hollow out a gourd and attach it to a pole, leaving the shell intact except for a hole just large enough to push a banana through. When a monkey stops to investigate, he will put his hand into the gourd to get the banana. But as soon as the monkey puts his hand on the banana, he's trapped. His hand and the banana will not fit through the hole. Because he can't imagine giving up the banana, his fate is sealed. He quite literally becomes a prisoner of his own mind.[1]

But we human beings do have awareness and choice. It is possible for us to decide to "let go" and create different choices for ourselves. But we create anxiety and dissatisfaction when we make our wants and desires the central focus for our happiness. We decide that we will be happy "when I get the new car," "when I can afford to travel," "when I lose fifteen pounds." If we postpone happiness "until . . .," what does that leave us *now*? Our feelings of restlessness and dissatisfaction keep us focusing narrowly ahead to our wants, forcing us to ignore the present. We live the "if only . . ." syndrome.

But, oddly enough, when we *do* fulfill one of these desires, our tendency is to look forward *again* to the next set of desires or wants that will bring us happiness. We become like a junkie on the prowl for the next "hit" of happiness—the next desire to fulfill. It's an absolute and sad certainty that we will never reach all the "requirements" we set for ourselves to achieve a sense of happiness.

Just how do we combat this "if only" mind trap so we can achieve a sense of peace? The answer is simple but not easy. We can focus on the enjoyment of the "now" in our life through *mindfulness*. We slow down our thoughts so we experience the moment as fully as possible through all our senses. For example, Stacy shares her idea of mindfulness with this excerpt from her journal:

> I am absorbed in the process of writing. As I lift my pen from the lined, white pad on my desk top, I stop to appreciate the here and now of what surrounds me. As I turn my head toward the window, I see the first snowfall of this winter season—the quiet delicacy of snowflakes falling on my deck. I hear and enjoy the sounds of a relaxing tape featuring sounds from nature. I feel the wonderful sensation of soft fur on my thighs as my cat, Miranda, provides wonderful company for me on this Saturday morning. I look at the top of my desk and appreciate the colors and textures of potpourri that fills a royal blue and gold-trimmed antique dish. To the right of the dish is a burgundy and blue pottery goblet that holds pens and pencils. Next to the goblet is the lovely, fluted glass of a two-inch-high candle holder that contains the delicate color and scent of a bayberry candle. I admire the wood grain of my walnut-stained desk top. A smile comes to my face as I look at the wood grain. I feel a sense of enjoyment and pleasure realizing that I stained and sanded this once hollow door mounted on two file cabinets that now serves as a desk top. My eyes also glance at the gold, heart-shaped paperweight—a birthday present from my dearest childhood friend.

Mindfulness requires us to look at the essence of the now and to feel the joy of the moment. The joy comes from the process of *doing* an activity rather than *finishing* the activity. But how do we make this major change in attitude from the "if only" mind trap?

For three weeks, make a point of picking out one activity that you can enjoy in a "mindful" way. It could be eating a dessert, taking a shower, petting your cat or dog, listening to music, walking in a park, or taking a bubble bath. Enjoy every nuance of the activity—its taste, smell, sound, sight, touch. Concentrate fully on the enjoyment of the now. It will take practice and, at first, some effort. But after three weeks, this process will become a habit, and you will have created a peaceful time for yourself that has many benefits.

The creation of peacefulness and serenity may produce feelings of gratitude and thankfulness as we realize the many blessings with which we are surrounded. It can teach us new ways of looking at the events of our lives, especially when we are dealing with high expectations. It can also calm us and relax us so we become better attuned to our needs and wants. As we become clearer about our needs and wants, we can then start learning how to ask for what we want, which is the subject of the next chapter.

CHAPTER FOURTEEN

||||||||||||||||||||||||||||||||||||||||||||||||||||||||||||||||||||||

Learning to Ask for What You Want

One of the most important and valuable skills we can learn in recovery is asking for what we want. Some of the experiences of other adult children may provide some insight on how this skill can be important to us.

Sandra's Story
 . . . the word escape *kept entering my mind.*

It was 9:20 A.M. As Sandra sat at her office desk that July morning, she kept thinking of the week-long trip she'd just taken with Bill—a motorcycle trip to Arkansas. She vividly recalled the second day of the trip. That afternoon they were on their way into Arkansas from Missouri. She could see her upper arms becoming steadily pinker as the sun bore down on them. The red of her tank top seemed an interesting contrast. The pavement kept passing beneath them; the noise of the cycle remained constant; the sun seemed fixed in the sky. She felt mesmerized. She remembers leaning forward and saying to Bill: "Let's just keep going. It's not that much farther to New Orleans."

"As I sat at my desk, the word *escape* kept entering my mind," Sandra recalls. "I knew I had wanted to escape when I took that trip—but from whom or what? I also knew I was trying to escape from something through my relationship with Bill. Deep down I knew this relationship wasn't the answer, but I hung on tightly anyway. But if this relationship wasn't the answer, what was?''

By November, her relationship with Bill became very rocky. By January, it was over. Sandra felt her world was collapsing.

A year and a half later, Sandra was attending lectures and seminars on adult children of alcoholics issues, reading every related self-help book she could get her hands on, and asking questions of people she felt she could trust. "I couldn't yet ask for help, but I *could* ask questions. I at least partially knew the answer to the question, who or what was I trying to escape? As hard as it was to admit, I realized in one of those 'blinding glimpses of the obvious' that I'd been trying to escape responsibility for my own life. What did I want to do with my life? What was my purpose? Where was I going?

"From the time I was eight, I'd known I'd wanted to become a nurse. But after being a nurse for two years, I realized that *wasn't* the answer. I was doing part-time nursing work on weekends (a financial necessity) in addition to my regular Monday through Friday job, and I was angry about having to do it.''

It's taken four years for Sandra to fully accept responsibility for her own life. From time to time she still occasionally finds herself wanting an easy way out—accepting passivity instead of action; retreating from situations rather than facing them; living in the future instead of mindfully engaging in the here and now. Does this sound at all familiar? By and large, however, she feels great joy that she has set a course for herself. She has goals, plans, hopes, and dreams. Some of these goals and dreams have been modified or altered in the last several years, including her plan to pursue a business certification program at a local university. But Sandra considers taking the business courses as a positive, since she discovered something about herself: the business program wasn't where she wanted to concentrate her career effort.

Certainly there are still pieces she's struggling with—including what career to pursue. But she is looking at different options until she finds the right niche, and she is enjoying the process along the way.

The Choice Is Yours

Excusing ourselves from responsibility does provide a gain of sorts (even though it's a negative gain): it prevents us from being blamed. But, at the same time, excusing ourselves from responsibility also prevents us from feeling good about ourselves—from feeling fulfilled, excited about our achievements, ideas, and goals. As we learn who we are and how we want to live each day, we can *create* our own choices. We can say good-bye to passivity and the feelings of helplessness and powerlessness. We can say good-bye to the feeling of *why bother? It won't work anyway.* We can know, learn, and truly believe that we deserve better, that we can choose our actions and responses. We can accept responsibility for our actions.

Each of us is blessed with the responsibility of who we become—though at times it may seem more like an unmanageable burden than a blessing. Blaming others for our unhappiness will not create solutions. Only we can create our own solutions. Certainly other people do affect us, but we give up our power when we let them control us, overwhelm us, shame us, or diminish us. Frustration and defeat are not natural for us. What does come naturally is: "If it's to be, it's up to me."

One way of taking responsibility is to ask for what you want. Asking for what you want is a powerful and positive way to develop greater self-confidence, feel better about yourself, and create what you want in your life.

Many aspects of our family history and the socialization process reinforce our tendencies not to ask for what we need. Many of us fear that we might be viewed as "not nice," "pushy," or "selfish." And in our alcoholic families, we may have learned early to adopt a survival mode, attempting to develop some control over our environment through denying feelings or shutting down emotionally. We may have frequently focused on things that needed to be done since we tended not to trust that people could be there for us. Living in this way, how could we have possibly asked for what we wanted?

Ironically, when we take responsibility for asking for what we want, we feel better about ourselves, which tends to create positive situations for all those around us. We begin to act from a sense of confidence rather than a sense of neediness. We become a positive example to others of how beneficial asking for what *we want* can be. Once we start this process, and continue to practice it and reinforce it, the more natural it becomes and the greater our sense of self-confidence and self-worth becomes.

In the following story, we'll show you how *not* asking for what you want can create ripples and waves that may have negative impact on many people. And then we'll look at how the same situation could be turned around to produce a positive outcome.

Gary's Story
The man yelled, "Good, I'm glad you won't be here anymore!"

As Gary walked toward the entrance of the junior high where he taught an extension class for a community college, he realized that something unusual was going on that night. There were lots of cars in the parking lot and many people in the building. When he neared the classroom, he noticed a number of his students sitting quietly at desks outside the classroom. Many were studying for the final exam they were to take that night. There was a junior high teacher sitting at the desk when Gary walked into his usual classroom. The teacher explained that parent-teacher conferences were in progress; Gary's class could come into the classroom at 6:20 P.M. It was 6:05 and Gary's class began at 6:30. When Gary stepped outside the classroom, a number of his students approached him, as always, to ask questions.

As Gary finished talking with the last student, he looked around and realized that in the middle of the area outside the classroom where his students had gathered sat a teacher and parent engaged in a conference. Before he could react to this, a man came up behind Gary, and in a very stern, angry voice asked if he was the extension class teacher. When Gary said yes, the man upbraided Gary in front of all of his students:

"What are you doing here with a conference going on? Can't you see the problems you've created? How many more classes will you be teaching here?" When Gary explained in a calm voice that this was the last class—a final exam—the man yelled, "Good, I'm glad you won't be here anymore!" and walked away.

Gary was dumbfounded. One of his students said to him, "I want you to know that when I got here earlier, I *asked* the junior high teacher if it would be all right if I sat here to study and she said, 'Yes, I only have one more conference; that's fine.'"

As the parent-teacher conference ended and Gary ushered his students into the classroom, the classroom teacher stopped Gary. "By the way," she said, "I'd really appreciate it if you'd put the chairs back in order at the end of your class. It takes me about twenty minutes to do that in the morning." Gary said he was surprised because he assumed that the janitors, who were still there when he left at 10:00 P.M., had cleaned and straightened the room. Gary was amazed because he'd been teaching the class for ten weeks and had never received a note or any communication from the teacher asking him to straighten chairs. She'd probably been really upset with Gary and the class for ten weeks and hadn't said a word!

"After the class settled in and began taking the final exam, I walked down to the main office to see if I could find the man who had spoken so angrily to me," Gary says. "I saw the man sitting at a desk and realized he was the principal of the school. I shared with him what the student had told me. He said he'd had a rough day and apologized. I thanked him and went back to the classroom."

Gary realized that there was an important lesson here. The junior high teacher *did* have the option to tell Gary's students that it would be a distraction for them to study outside the classroom and she would appreciate if they'd use another classroom. Instead, the teacher sat with the parent, became increasingly angry, and finally expressed her anger to the principal. If she had asked for what she wanted in the first place, a clearly tired and frustrated principal would have had one less problem, and Gary and his students would not have become targets for his rage. Likewise, if the junior high teacher had asked Gary to put the chairs back in order rather than storing her frustration for ten weeks, it would have been easier on her. And it would have quickly solved the problem.

"Although these were not exactly pleasant experiences for me," Gary says, "they offered valuable insight into the importance of asking for what you want."

Asking for what you want *can* be frightening and difficult to do. Gary was asking for what he wanted when he talked to the principal. Although Gary was uncomfortable, he could not let the principal treat him and his students in a disrespectful manner without voicing his concern. Gary did what he needed to do for himself and his students. He felt good about taking care of himself.

When you ask for what you want, you do take the risk that you won't get it. When we start asserting ourselves, as Gary did, we are changing the patterns of our relationships—especially with those we're closest to. That can be unsettling, uncomfortable, even threatening. Any kind of change—even positive change—rocks the boat and causes feelings of anxiety.

CHAPTER FIFTEEN

||||||||||||||||||||||||||||||||||||||||||||||||||||||||||||||||||||||||||

Practicing How to Ask for What You Want

Many of us are so accustomed to not asking for what we want that we tend to accept a low hum of dissatisfaction in many of our relationships. How can we know what better relationships are like if we've not experienced them? It's just like anything else in life that we've never experienced. Though we might try and imagine the sensation of hang gliding, few of us could actually undergo that feeling unless we'd caught the air currents ourselves. Likewise, how can we possibly understand the depth of the grief that accompanies the loss of a parent until we've undergone the loss ourselves? How can we know the sensations of what a healthy relationship feels like unless we've had one?

When we start to experience a healthy relationship, it may feel uncomfortable since it's so different from any of our previous experiences. And when things feel uncomfortable, it's natural to desire the return of a previously known comfort level, even if that comfort level includes pain.

So let's begin to feel the joy of getting what we want in small, step-by-step ways, so we can begin to get a sense of how getting what we want feels.

If not asking for what we want is an established pattern, we'll need to consciously build a new habit. This will take effort, time, and patience. The progression may not be a steady upward slope; it may include plateaus and lines that zigzag backward instead of forward at times. Even though such un-predictable movement can be frustrating, it is natural.

Treat yourself kindly in this process, and remember that you've had many years of practice in building your automatic patterns. Changing those patterns can take some time. But it can be done, and the results will be worth the effort.

A good first step to practice is asking yourself what *you* want. Here are some sample questions one person asked:

- How can I live so as to not feel so rushed all the time?
- How can I fit an interesting class into my schedule?
- How can I buy that scarf that I've wanted for a long time?
- How can I see a good friend more frequently?
- How can I squeeze in thirty minutes twice a week to soak in a hot tub?
- How can I spend more time enjoying nature?

One of the most difficult parts of this is finding time to do what we need for ourselves. Somehow other people, activities, and events always seem to come before our wants.

EXERCISE FOR GETTING
THE MOST OUT OF LIFE

Quickly, brainstorm and jot down a list of ten things you'd like in your life.

Review the list and find one item to which you have the strongest emotional response, and brainstorm ways to get this item into your life.

For instance, if that soak in a hot bubble bath twice a week would feel glorious to you, how can you make sure you get it?

- You might get up earlier in the morning to enjoy it.
- You might ask a neighbor to watch the children for a half hour twice a week so you can soak, and then offer to do the same for her.
- You might ask your husband or wife or significant other if he or she could watch the children as you enjoy your soak.
- You might make sure that two times a week your outside activities won't keep you out beyond 9:00 P.M. so you still have one full hour to soak before bedtime.
- If you feel stuck for workable solutions, call several friends and get their ideas. Or you might get several friends together and help each other brainstorm ideas for getting what each of you wants.

How to Get Started

Start your process of asking for what you want by thinking of your relationship with your best friend.

- Are you completely satisfied with the relationship?

- Are any parts of you dissatisfied, "shut down," or frustrated in this relationship?
- Have you purposely not said some things that might have rocked the boat? Do these issues still bother you?

Take a sheet of paper or your journal and begin writing about your friendship.

- What needs does this friendship satisfy?
- What haven't you asked for that would make this friendship even more satisfying?

Write this down. It's not necessary to act on any of these thoughts at this point. In fact, initially, that may seem pretty frightening and overwhelming. For the time being, just write down your thoughts. Then give yourself time away from these thoughts so your unconscious mind can assimilate your wants and needs and determine how you might best get them.

The process is different for each of us. But in a matter of hours, days, or weeks, you will perhaps know with a very crystalized sense of certainty how and when you can ask your friend for what you want. When you feel ready to do it, the opportunity will appear, and you'll feel comfortable in the process.

The first step is giving yourself permission to have what you want and deserve. *Then actually taking the necessary steps to make sure it happens* is crucial. If you aren't important enough to yourself to complete this first step, then the following steps will be useless. You deserve more happiness and joy in your life no matter what those old messages may tell you.

Pick one item now that you want in your life and prepare to welcome the sense of joy that will come your way when you experience it.

CHAPTER SIXTEEN

Trusting in the Outcome

Taking the steps of asking for what you want *will* initially feel awkward. You may feel a knot of fear in your stomach as you summon the courage to verbalize your thoughts, feelings, and needs. Practicing what you will say or do is one way to calm your fears and give yourself more self-confidence. Another way is perhaps even harder for most adult children, but extremely important: trusting in the outcome.

It's an amazing phenomenon, but seemingly true: when you make one major change in your life, other changes seem to just start happening. Glenn noticed this when he started to attend aerobics classes regularly. About six months after beginning this exercise routine, he started to change his diet, regularly eating whole grains and fruit. It wasn't a conscious effort or an abrupt one. Many people have experienced this phenomenon. So if you're feeling overwhelmed or hopeless about the number of changes or the magnitude of the one or two changes in your life you'd like to make, be heartened by the experience of others. Just direct your energy at first toward *one* change you'd like to make in your life. Remember, too, that it's easier to add something new into your routine and habit patterns than to eliminate an old pattern.

To get changes underway, you may want to pick something first that you can add—perhaps aerobic exercises, relaxation exercises, meditation, or quiet time just for you. Also remember that once you've begun this activity, get support or help in any way you can, especially for the first twenty-one days. Many experts agree that once you've practiced a new habit or pattern for twenty-one consecutive days, you've probably won the battle. After twenty-one days, you should have created a new habit.

But one change often takes longer to occur in our lives: the development of trust. After years of consciously working toward developing new habits, we may begin experiencing small glimpses of what trust can mean in our lives. For many of us, it's a sense of calmness and joy—a sense that things *will* work out. And it seems to include both big and small events. Perhaps a great part of developing this sense of trust is developing trust and faith in yourself as well as in a Higher Power who will guide you. Perhaps it's a result of giving yourself relaxation time each day so you can be more aware of your inner voice. Perhaps it's regularly trusting your intuition—paying attention to the signals and letting yourself be guided by them. Ironically, when you do trust and don't push or get anxious, things have a remarkable way of working out.

Larry's Story
. . . I just let go of fear and worry.

Larry and his date were enjoying good food and conversation at an Italian restaurant. They'd planned to go to a movie at a theater seven miles away but became so engrossed in conversation that they lost track of time. When they realized the time, they signalled for the waiter, but realized that they'd probably be late since the movie started in five minutes. Since Larry's car was parked closer, he drove. Ordinarily, he would have felt rather uptight about being late. He could also tell his date was somewhat concerned about being late, which normally would have added to his anxiety. But Larry felt a sense of peacefulness and didn't worry.

"There was nothing I could do to change the circumstances, so I just let go of fear and worry," he says. "I dropped Sandy off to get in line for tickets, found a parking space, and joined her. As we walked down the aisle of the theater, the opening credits were just coming on for the movie. All we'd missed were the previews of other movies. Our timing was perfect."

In the next example, you'll see how a trigger point—money in this case—almost automatically caused anxiety for Sally.

Sally's Story

I kept thinking to myself, What's wrong with you? You should be panicking.

"For two and one-half years after my separation and divorce I'd had renters so I could handle my condominium mortgage payments. I'd also found a part-time job as a hairdresser to bring in additional dollars," recalls Sally. Two years into this process Sally decided that even though she loved the condo location, it was too much of a struggle financially, and she put the condo up for sale. There were no takers. There was a glut of condominiums on the market, and Sally's unit did not have an assumable mortgage. After six months, Sally took her condo off the market.

A year later, after her renter moved out, Sally decided she wanted the place to herself for a while. Since her salary had increased, she would just be able to make it financially if she stayed with her part-time hairdresser work as well as her full-time job. The room that had previously been her renter's room became her office where she worked on jewelry designs in her spare time. She surrounded her work area with items that she loved—plants, photographs, quotations. Her desk became an early morning retreat, where she developed a ritual that she loved: she listened to a favorite radio station, drank coffee, and planned her day.

Six months later, she realized that, according to her divorce agreement, she had approximately a year and a half to come up with enough money to buy out her ex-husband or sell the condo. She realized she'd have to find another renter to save the money she needed. Sally placed an ad and received a response almost immediately from someone who seemed perfect. On the day he was supposed to move in, he never showed up, and Sally learned he'd decided against it. She was disappointed. By the time she placed another ad and someone moved in, she would have lost six weeks. She did place another ad but had no luck.

Normally, she would have been extremely worried, frustrated, and frantic. But for some reason, she remained calm. She didn't know why.

"I kept thinking to myself, *What's wrong with you? You should be panicking.* But I didn't. Since it was close to Thanksgiving, I decided I'd wait until after the holidays to run another ad. In the meantime, I continued to enjoy my office at home. I really did cherish that special work area and realized how ambivalent I felt about giving it up."

When Sally learned that a major retailer was interested in the jewelry she'd designed, she realized what her lack of panic was all about. With these sales, she'd have additional income. She'd also need her work area now to design more jewelry. Her trust was indeed validated. When she realized this, she felt an even greater sense of calm and serenity. Somehow, it was like a snowball effect. The more she trusted, the more things seemed to work out and the more she trusted. She much preferred this cycle over the old one that involved anxiety, worry, fear—and more anxiety, worry, and fear!

Keith's Story
Trusting the Outcome

Keith's story provides another example of how trusting the outcome can work. Recently Keith received a registered letter from his employer saying that he'd be laid off. He was totally unprepared for this news. He called his employer, who explained the company was hiring two new employees. Because of this, they had to notify all part-time personnel of a layoff. Of the three part-timers, Keith was lowest on the seniority ladder. Keith's boss indicated that with the hiring of two new full-time people, probably only one part-time employee would be hired back.

"After talking with my boss, I realized that two very distinct feelings had come over me. One was worry: how would I make it without my additional part-time salary? But the other feeling was one that surprised me: it was one of relief. Although I'd enjoyed the part-time job, I was feeling burned out from working two jobs.''

Though he feels uneasy about what will happen after the layoff or where additional income might come from, he knows that somehow things will work out. There's even a part of him that's excited about the new directions that seem to be opening up for him. Keith would welcome change.

''For the last three years when I've gone in to have my taxes prepared, I've been asked if anything has changed. My answer has always been no. Someday I'd like to go in and say, 'Well, yes, as a matter of fact, I'm accepting a new job and moving to England next month.' ''

Those exact words won't fit, but certainly things are changing. And Keith knows they will keep changing for the better, as they will for you as you continue on your path of recovery.

As we continue on the recovery path, we know that letting go and trusting that all will be well doesn't mean that we don't put effort into the process. The Quakers have a beautiful phrase: ''Pray with moving feet.'' In other words, we need to invest all our effort and energy to make sure that we achieve our goals and dreams. But once we've prayed with moving feet, we do need to let go and trust that what happens will not only be right for us, but will happen when the time is right.

CHAPTER SEVENTEEN

Understanding and Appreciating Synchronicity

Trusting in the outcome will not only provide a stronger sense of peacefulness in our lives. It can also lead us to a greater appreciation of a process in our lives that Swiss psychologist Carl Jung has termed *synchronicity*. Let's look at how this concept works.

Have you ever felt as if you were a day late and a dollar short when a special opportunity presented itself? Did it ever seem to you that no matter how hard you worked at something, how much time, money, and effort you spent on a project, that it just wouldn't come together the way you wanted?

On the other hand, have you ever felt that there were days or weeks in your life when you could do no wrong? Have you ever experienced the sense of power that comes with having a business deal work out perfectly when everybody, including your boss, was skeptical?

Don's Story
How Does It Feel to Have the Job You Really Want Handed to You?

Don had an experience like this. He was cleaning out a closet in his house and found a photograph of himself with two high school friends he hadn't seen in twenty years. He reminisced briefly about some of his antics back then, wondered how his friends were doing, and put the photograph back in the box.

Within the next two weeks, he ran into both of them. They got together for lunch and started talking about some of those memories.

"As it turned out, one of my friends had started a business and just happened to be looking for a person with my kind of skills," Don recalls. "I was thinking about leaving my job anyway but just hadn't gotten around to looking elsewhere."

How does it feel to have your next job, the kind of job you really want, handed to you? Coincidence you say? Dumb luck maybe? Maybe, maybe not.

If you have ever been thinking really hard about someone and then had the phone ring and it is that person on the other end of the line, you have had a brief experience with a concept called *synchronicity*. Jung, in his book titled *Synchronicity*, attempts to describe the phenomena of synchronicity and to place parameters around the measurement of such events:

> The philosophical principle that underlies our conception of natural law is **causality**.* But if the connection between cause and effect turns out to be only statistically valid and only relatively true, then the causal principle is only of relative use for explaining natural processes and therefore presupposes the existence of one or more other factors which would be necessary for an explanation. This is as much as to say that the connection of events may in certain circumstances be other than causal, and requires another principle of explanation.[1]

Jung's basic premise is that there is a relationship between a person thinking about a friend and the friend calling. But in terms of traditional scientific methodology, we don't have any statistically reliable method of measuring why these events occur and why they are important or connective. The difficulty is that we don't have a simple explanation for synchronicity, nor are the conditions or events usually reproducible in a laboratory. Given the difficulty of proving that certain events are

---

Causality means other than, or supplementary to, the laws of chance.

more than chance but not readily reducible to a theory such as
A+B=C, how is it that we can begin to understand synchronicity? Several stories follow that illustrate the concept perhaps
better than it can be explained.

Karen's Story
*One morning I found a job description on the bulletin board
that made my heart jump.*

Karen had been job hunting for about six months. She had
applied for several jobs that she found in the paper but was
feeling frustrated and upset because she hadn't even gotten a
first interview. She kept trying to keep a good attitude. But
because of all the problems at her current job, she was running
out of patience. Karen said that her lack of a college degree
was hurting her chances in finding another job, but she didn't
make enough money to pay for school and her other expenses.
She felt stuck and scared.

"I worked in a company with about one hundred fifty employees," Karen says. "I had talked with several people in
other divisions hoping there might be a position for me in one
of the other departments, or perhaps someone would know of
another job or hear something interesting.

"One morning I noticed a job description on the bulletin
board that made my heart jump. From the looks of it, it might
have been the perfect job for me. The real problem was that
they asked for a college degree that I didn't have. What could
I do?

"About half an hour later, I overheard some co-workers talking about the job I was interested in. Apparently, the supervisor was absolutely desperate to fill the position since it had
been six months since the former employee had left.

"I gathered my courage and called the personnel office, saying I was interested in the job. I asked if not having a degree
would be a problem. The personnel manager, Allison, and I
discussed specific tasks involved in the position, and then Allison agreed to call me back with an answer to my question
about the degree.

"Allison did call back to say that my experience was an acceptable substitute and asked me to come in for an interview.

"I was eventually offered the job. Not only was I feeling great about getting a new position, but it turned out that my new employer was also willing to reimburse employees who took courses to improve their skills. I was well on my way to getting my college degree and happily employed as well."

Just a neat little turn of events that happened to turn out in Karen's favor? Sure, you could chalk it up to good luck. But what are the chances that your prospective employer would be willing to waive a major qualification difficulty because the company needed someone with your skills and the company needed you now? What are the chances of finding an employer willing to help pay for the education you need to even be considered for the job? When Karen added up these facts, she attributed her good fortune to a lot more than chance.

Bob's Story
They were all in a deep discussion about "the book."

Another story that illustrates a more-than-chance series of events happened to Bob. Bob walked into his favorite bookstore one day and happened to pick up a self-help book. He read the introduction, thought he might really enjoy reading it, but for several reasons he decided not to purchase it. He kept thinking about how expensive the book was and about how many books he had at home on similar subjects. Bob also thought that he could probably borrow it from a library. He left the bookstore feeling disappointed, but he also felt he had made a good decision.

"When I arrived home, I looked through my mail," Bob recalls. "One of my favorite magazines had arrived, and when I glanced through the index, I realized that the review for the month was on *that* book. I immediately read the review. It was unusual for that particular reviewer to have the same tastes as me. But this review was positively glowing.

"The next day at work I decided to eat lunch in the cafeteria with some of my co-workers rather than eat it at my desk as I usually did. I purchased my lunch and went to the table where they were sitting. They were all deep in a discussion about 'the book.' I was beginning to wonder how many more times I would encounter a reminder of how much I wanted to purchase that book.''

That same night Bob received a call from his friend Stan. Several weeks earlier, Bob and Stan had agreed to go to the car races. Stan wanted to confirm their weekend outing but, in passing, also said he had just bought a great book that Bob would like.

You already know which book it was.

The very next day, Bob returned to the bookstore and purchased a copy. He had had enough of these ''reminders'' and just accepted that he was ''supposed to'' read that book. He found the book to be a pivotal influence in his recovery program.

Living in the Present: Practicing Mindfulness

Perhaps the most important concept that these ''coincidental'' events share is the idea of mindfulness. If we are awake and paying attention to what is going on in our lives, if we are living mindfully, we begin to see or sense the patterns that occasionally occur. Some of the patterns are bolder than others, like Bob's book incident. We can easily see them and understand the messages contained within them. Others are more subtle. We can see them only if we are really paying attention and living mindfully. It is these subtler events that can be the most helpful, but we have to be paying close attention to notice them.

In Chapter Thirteen on mindfulness (pages 101–103), we learned about the spiritual nature of living in the moment, of really being present in our lives. Living in the ''now'' allows us the opportunity to feel the power of the present rather than being lost in the pain of past memories or in worry about times, places, and events that haven't yet occurred. Noticing the events of here-and-now offers insight into our abilities to cope and provides the chance to heal old wounds and memories. Take the case of Sarah and a recent visit she made to her hometown. By paying attention to her here-and-now instinct of wishing to visit a favorite childhood beach, she experienced a series of events that brought her joy. By reliving some of the moments of innocence, sensory experience, and happiness of her childhood, she helped heal the wounded, inner child that most of us adult children of alcoholics carry with us into our adult lives.

Sarah's Story

To my amazement, he asked, "Would you like to come in and see it?"

Sarah and her friend, Gene, were driving to the Chicago area to attend the wedding of Sarah's nephew. They had taken a few extra days of vacation to explore the area where Sarah had grown up. It would be especially fun for Gene, since he had only driven through Chicago and hadn't really seen much of it.

"Since it was early spring, I suggested that we drive to Evanston, the suburb where I was born and raised," Sarah recalls. "The drive would be lovely this time of year, and it would be fun to see the beautiful homes and mansions that lined the 'North Shore' of Lake Michigan. When we drove into the suburb of Kenilworth, I asked Gene if he would mind stopping and walking with me on a little beach where I had frequently gone with my sister and grandmother. Warm, happy memories of walking barefoot down the cement sidewalks of the tree-lined street leading to the beach flooded back to me. I remembered Grandmother always carrying a bag packed with beach towels, bananas, and, one of the highlights of the outing, Mounds candy bars. Though the beach was smaller than I remembered, it was still a lovely, peaceful spot.

"Gene then asked if I would like to walk the four blocks I had walked as a child to Grandmother's old apartment. I was thrilled. I hadn't walked that route for thirty years. We passed the lovely old churchyard where the poet Eugene Field was buried, and we continued on to cross the railroad tracks in front of Grandmother's old apartment. The park where my grandmother and I had spent hours watching the trains go by now had a house on it, but otherwise, the area looked much the same.

"As we neared the block of little stores near Grandmother's old apartment, I wondered if I would remember exactly where Grandmother had lived. Her apartment had been above Mr. Driscoll's meat market, and I smiled as I remembered Grandmother preparing our favorite dinner of cottage cheese, tomato and mayonnaise salad, cube steaks, and lumpy mashed potatoes. Staying up late watching Fahey Flynn and P. J. Hoff on the local CBS news station came to mind, as did nights spent under the stars sleeping on the old glider on Grandmother's back porch."

As Sarah tentatively opened the apartment building door, she smiled and said hello to a man opening his mailbox. She remembered thinking that perhaps he was the dentist who had an office in the building. Gene and Sarah climbed the steps of the apartment building and walked to the end of the corridor. As they turned to walk back down the small hallway, Sarah noticed that the man who had been at the mailbox was putting a key in the door to her grandmother's former apartment. He looked up and asked if he could be of assistance. Sarah felt a lump in her throat as she said, "This was my grandmother's apartment that we visited as kids, and I haven't seen it for close to thirty years."

"To my amazement, he asked, 'Would you like to come in and see it?' Would I ever! I looked to the left as I entered, expecting to see Grandmother's TV in the far corner of the room and the big, old wing chair with the lace doilies on the arms. Though the look of the apartment was now far more contemporary because of the furnishings, it had essentially remained the same."

Sarah returned to the present moment and heard the owner comment on how much he liked the area. He had intended to stay in the apartment only a year or two, but he'd now been there five years. Sarah was trying hard to listen and respond, but part of her was an eight-year-old sitting on her grandmother's double foldout bed and watching the news.

"As Gene and I thanked our host and walked down the apartment building steps, we turned and stared at each other. Gene then spoke out loud the very thoughts that had been going through my mind: 'Wasn't it odd that the man who lived in your grandmother's former apartment had been returning to his apartment in the afternoon on a Thursday? What a strange coincidence!' "

Sarah smiled and shook her head. The odds against such a thing happening were astronomical. But lately, more and more, such experiences had been happening in her life. Or maybe it wasn't a matter of there being more of such experiences; perhaps she was just noticing and paying attention to such experiences now. She chalked it up to one more example of the concept of synchronicity.

"I still feel a sense of awe and amazement when I think back to seeing Grandmother's apartment again after a thirty-year absence. The positive memories associated with this 'coincidence' remain a source of strength and delight to me. I give thanks for this experience and others in my life that I would term *synchronistic*."

Understanding and appreciating the concept of synchronicity has helped Sarah attain a sense of peacefulness and serenity. Although some of us may want black-and-white answers and not understand how, specifically, this synchronicity concept works, just letting ourselves appreciate it rather than analyze it can be a helpful experience.

The more open and trusting we are in the process, the more readily we experience the synchronous events in our lives. Synchronous events seem to flow more easily if we are open to positive expectations and experiences. And as we progress in our recovery, we tend to develop a sense of positive expectancy, which lends itself well to the understanding and appreciation of the concept of synchronicity.

Synchronicity also has an aspect of faith or belief in what the future will bring. Take the story of Owen and his wife Marisa.

Owen and Marisa's Story

Following the Inner Voice to Success

Owen was an executive vice-president in a start-up software manufacturing company in Omaha, Nebraska. Creative and entrepreneurial, Owen had landed his current job through a former employee from another small start-up business that had closed its doors for financial reasons.

Owen had long harbored a dream of starting his own computer distributorship. Aware of unfilled needs in certain niches in the marketplace, Owen kept his dream alive by continually working on a business plan for himself. He planned to work for three more years to save enough money to fund the first eighteen months of a start-up business, hoping he could make it profitable by then.

Marisa, Owen's wife, hoped that Owen would settle down and earn a living for a while, since she was tired of his bouncing around from job to job. Marisa was an office manager for a large advertising company. She had started at the agency as a receptionist eight years earlier, and, through working very diligently, she had been promoted every other year. But her dream was to go to college and get a degree in organizational development. If Owen was willing, she hoped to quit her job soon and go to school full time. At the very least, she intended to take evening classes during the coming fall quarter.

Both Owen and Marisa were adult children of alcoholics. Both were in recovery programs, and, though there were many problems in their lives and in their relationship, they worked diligently to try to talk things through. For the moment, they were succeeding.

In August, Marisa decided to take an evening class that fall at the local university. But something kept nagging at her that it wasn't the time to go to school yet. Even trying to register for one class proved difficult. On the way to register one evening, she had a flat tire. Then she tried to mail in her registration only to have it come back to her two weeks later, because it had been sent to the wrong address. She tried again to register in person, only to be told that the class was full and she would have to be put on a waiting list. There was no guarantee that she would make it into the class even if she attended and did the work in the first two weeks.

"Throughout the process of trying to register, I began to feel obsessed with getting into the class," Marisa says. "Though I was somewhat familiar with the concept of synchronicity, I also felt afraid that if I didn't start school that fall, I would never start it. My insecurity and need for control were rearing their heads in a big way. So despite feeling as if I were doing something foolish, I registered for the class. When another student dropped out after two weeks and I was accepted, I felt elated and could hardly wait to tell Owen.

"When I arrived home that evening, I raced into the house to tell Owen the good news. But the look on his face stopped me cold. Owen said the company he worked for was reorganizing and moving to Phoenix in six weeks. I was stunned. I felt all along that I was getting signals that I shouldn't sign up for school, but I had ignored that intuitive voice. Now I would have to withdraw from class and would lose half the cost of registration. That made me very upset."

Had Marisa listened to that persistent little voice and taken note of the obstacles placed between her and her desire, she would have saved time, effort, and money. Instead she chose, as many of us might, to ignore the information and go ahead with her plan. She vowed to pay closer attention the next time things seemed to happen in a consistent pattern. She didn't have to wait very long.

Since he had heard the news, Owen had had a bad feeling about the impending move and his position in the company. There had been a lot of talk from a certain group of investors about taking over management, and Owen was feeling very uncertain about his future.

"Though I was feeling scared, I kept my thoughts to myself," Owen says. "Marisa and I had fought many times about my desire to work in small, start-up companies. I wanted to be a part of making a company really grow from the bottom up, but my dream had been shattered several times by the reality of bankruptcy, politics, and mismanagement. Rather than possibly upset Marisa, I spent a lot of time working on my business plan and talking with friends about my fears.''

Marisa also had a bad feeling about the move. She decided not to give notice at work until two weeks before she was scheduled to leave town and move to her new home. This time she was going to listen to that little voice and not jump before she was ready.

Four weeks after the move had been announced, Owen was called into the president's office. The investors had made their move and had fired all of the top management, including Owen. He was given his severance check and told to clean out his desk. Angry and frustrated, he packed up his belongings and left.

If Owen was angry, Marisa was mortified. This was Owen's fourth job in three years. She was upset with the constant changes and apparent instability of his work. She was beginning to think he would never settle down and produce a steady income. Though she made a good salary, it didn't cover all of their monthly expenses. Owen's severance pay would cover them for a month or two, but then what? His last bout with unemployment had eaten up their savings, and they still had several outstanding loans. Her dream of returning to school full time was out the window.

After several months of serious thought, Owen decided it was time to pursue his dream of creating his own business. Though he was also scared about their finances, he felt that this was his chance to pursue his dream and that somehow, some way, things would work out.

When Owen told Marisa about his desire to create his own company, she thought it was the right thing to do. Since Owen had lost his job, Marisa had talked with several people in the ad agency where she worked about looking for a new job herself. She wanted to find something similar to her current job but wanted a 20 percent raise in pay. If she could get that salary, at least they could pay the mortgage and utilities. She also knew that her internal voice hadn't screamed at the idea of Owen starting up his own company. If things that Owen needed to start his business came easily to him, it meant to her that he was doing the right thing. If she got a new job easily, it meant she was doing the right thing. This time she was going to work with this synchronicity concept and be aware of any messages that appeared to form a pattern.

Marisa started looking for a new job in January, and by March she had secured a new position in another ad agency with not a 20 percent raise but a 45 percent hike in salary!

When Owen filed incorporation papers in March, a lawyer friend who owed him a favor did the service for no charge, a blessing in Owen's mind and one more sign in Marisa's mind that they were doing the right thing. When the lawyer learned that Owen was looking for a line of credit at a bank, he sent Owen to another client of his, a banker who specialized in small business loans. Owen was able to get a small but crucial line of credit without the usual hassle or demand for collateral. By May, the business was doing well enough that Owen began contributing to the household budget again. Even a skeptical scientist like Owen had to admit that they seemed to be "tuned in" to something that kept giving them signs of when to proceed and when to back off.

After a year, Marisa and Owen had paid off most of their old debts; after two years, Marisa had saved enough money of her own to pursue her dream. She quit her job and went back to school full time.

Owen thinks that he would have invited another firing or crisis of some kind if he hadn't chosen to follow his inner sense. For the concept of synchronicity to be useful, you must believe that the incidents of your life are more than just random occurrences or capriciousness in an unfair world.

If the idea that messages are just waiting to be unfolded to you by the universe doesn't sit well with you, at least be willing to try mindfulness as discussed in Chapter Thirteen (pages 101–103). Information and insight are important when you are trying to create choices in your life. Whether an event is chance or a "message" doesn't matter if you are aware of the possible consequences of the situation and can use the event or information to take you further down the path to your goals and dreams. If you take the attitude that everything that is happening is important, you will be able to find the silver lining in the events of your life.

PART THREE

Activities

CHAPTER EIGHTEEN

||||||||||||||||||||||||||||||||||||||||||||||||||||||||||||||||||||||||

Introduction to Guidance Mechanisms

You've probably invested a lot of time learning what it means to be an adult child of an alcoholic. Most likely you've read books, listened to tapes, and attended seminars or group meetings. Or perhaps you've gained insight and understanding through a combination of these methods. After immersing yourself in this information, you may have reached a point where you asked: "Okay, I've explored much of the background on being an adult child; now what do I *do* about it?"

That question is usually asked with a tinge of frustration. Usually by the time you ask it, you see clearly how adult child patterns influence many areas of your life. And you want to change—now.

That's exactly why the information that follows is included. These chapters will provide you with a variety of practical, specific options that have worked successfully for many adult children. Certainly this is not an "all or nothing" process. Don't feel that all of these options are a must for you. But do consider which of the practical options that follow might work in your life, and then make a thirty-day commitment to try at least one.

As many adult children have learned, when one change is made, others seem to follow naturally. Exercising regularly frequently leads to changes in nutritional patterns; relaxation exercises might naturally lead to meditation; or creative visualization exercises might lead to the use of affirmations. The important thing is to concentrate on making one, small, positive change in your life, as Karen has done.

Karen's Story
Prisons of Our Own Making

Karen was surprised and pleased to hear from Steve early Thursday afternoon at work. They talked for a few moments, and then he asked about her school schedule that night, what time she usually got home, and if he could call her. Karen felt pleased that she would hear from him later that evening. But her mind raced to the question: *I wonder if there's something specific he wants to talk about?* And the next question that surfaced brought old, negative feelings bubbling to the surface: *I wonder if he's going to tell me he doesn't want to see me anymore?* Sadness and fear rushed in from all sides. Karen felt a hard knot in her stomach and began analyzing everything that had been said the last time they were together.

About ten minutes into this process of spiraling doubt and fear, she reminded herself: *Karen, you're being ridiculous. Why couldn't he just as easily want to call you to ask you out for this weekend or discuss an idea for his business?* Even though these rational thoughts surfaced, they were quickly carried away by the growing tide of negativity and self-doubt. As her friend Gloria said, "I can jump into the gutter and swim around in the muck just about as well as anyone." And was Karen ever doing a top-notch job of it!

"When I left work to attend my class, I realized that on a scale of one to ten, my energy level and enthusiasm would have been lucky to reach three," Karen recalls. "I became angry with myself for letting these thoughts color and interfere with my studies. Yet, they certainly did for the first half of the class. After that, however, I was able to concentrate on the present moment and forget about the expected phone call."

When Karen got home, she jumped into her pajamas, washed her face, and tried some deep breathing exercises and relaxation techniques. She repeated to herself: *What will be, will be; there's nothing I can do about it.* She felt fairly calm when she heard the phone ring and picked it up. About ten minutes into the conversation, Karen asked Steve in as casual a tone as she could muster: "Was there a specific reason you wanted to talk tonight?"

He said, "Yes, when I called you this morning, I wanted to ask you out for Saturday night. Then when I got home and heard the message you'd left on my answering machine, I wondered if you were referring to me, to you, or to us?"

"That afternoon I had left a message on his answering machine about a beautiful meditation I had read that I immediately wished to share with him," Karen says. "It concerned a man who had recently been released from prison. After his release, one of the first things he did was to walk back and forth across the pressure plate of the bus station door. He wanted to be the one to have control over opening and closing the door. Although onlookers laughed at him, he didn't care. He appreciated the opportunity to go where he wanted when he wanted. He had much in common with people who have been trapped in prisons of their own making. We all have, in one way or another, prisons of our own—sometimes of our own making. I thought it was an interesting metaphor."

Steve had obviously been doing some of the same wondering and analyzing that Karen had been doing—he wondered what she had meant by referring to that quote. How ironic that he'd experienced some of what Karen had experienced and how ironic, in retrospect, that Karen had left a message earlier in the day about the prisons we create for ourselves.

The bars Karen had constructed earlier in the day with her thoughts were as immobilizing as any jail cell. Though she could shake her head and laugh after she had hung up the phone that night, Karen felt frustrated and upset with herself for having fallen back into old, negative thought patterns.

But Karen also had been aware of what she was doing and had consciously fought the negative thought patterns. Though she hadn't mastered them, at least she had put up some resistance. The next time something similar occurs, she knows she can do a better job with it.

The Right Stuff

Although changing habitual negative thought patterns will take work, it can be done. On the road of our recovery we have all made changes that have been a struggle. And most recovering people agree that the struggle has been worth it.

Working with some of the techniques we're discussing in this book will aid in this process. When we *let* ourselves do deep breathing and relaxation exercises and repeat the phrase "What will be, will be," we *do* feel more relaxed and peaceful. In this process we are utilizing our right brain capabilities. As many people have pointed out, including Dr. Herbert Benson and William Proctor in their book, *Your Maximum Mind*, utilizing our right brain can be a key to changing ingrained thought patterns and habits.

As Benson and Proctor write:

> The problem we all face is that certain modules in the brain are so strong and their patterns so deeply ingrained, that they tend to control others. In particular, this is a problem that seems to have developed many times in the relation between the left and right hemispheres. The left side of the brain—with its powerful abilities to analyze and make convincing inferences—may be portrayed in this context as a kind of "little dictator" over the right side. Many of our intuitive and creative functions, as well as much information that we need to know and use in changing our lives for the better, have in effect been enslaved by our rational left hemispheres. You might say we have become prisoners of the left sides of our brains.
>
> So our goal can be characterized as a sort of inner, mental revolution: We must overthrow the hegemony of the left hemisphere and allow the right to break free and assume its full stature in the thinking process. In this way we can hope to open the door to beneficial change and growth in our lives.[1]

According to Benson and Proctor, we are able to stop following the habitual "wired" pathways of our brains and "rewire'' our brains to create new pathways. Each of the following chapters in Section Three of this book describes one or more techniques that can be beneficial in this ''rewiring'' process.

- Exercise (Chapter Nineteen)
- Subliminal techniques (Chapter Twenty)
- Relaxation exercises, guided imagery, and meditation (Chapter Twenty-One)
- Visualization techniques (Chapter Twenty-Two)
- Affirmations (Chapter Twenty-Three)
- Journaling (Chapter Twenty-Four)

First, let's start with exercise.

CHAPTER NINETEEN

‖‖‖

Energizing Yourself
Through Exercise

If you're like many people, you're probably tensing up already at the thought of a regular exercise program. You're probably wondering how you could ever find the time and energy to fit one more thing into an already jammed schedule. But give yourself an opportunity to experience the benefits you'll gain by trying a regular exercise program for at least thirty days. You'll have more energy; you'll also feel more positive and better about yourself. So although you're giving up some time in your schedule for an exercise program, you will find that because of a more positive attitude and increased energy, you will be just as productive—if not more so. Let's take a look at Mary's experience to see how an exercise program worked for her.

Mary's Story
It Began on the Fourth of July

When Mary woke up that morning, she knew something was different. It was July Fourth. The thought came into her head, *This is my day of independence too. I've spent years of my life worrying about my weight. No longer do I want to expend time and energy in the morning worrying about whether the waistband on my skirt will feel too tight; whether my jacket will feel too constricting around my upper arms. I want to put my energy into constructive, positive activities and ideas. Enough of*

138

this incredible amount of energy I've put into worrying over weight for so many years!

"That day, I went to an aerobics class at a health club near where I work," Mary says. "I felt self-conscious, fat, and worried that I couldn't keep up through an hour-long aerobics workout. But I was determined that I would keep going. That was two and one-half years ago. I'm still working out three days a week. I now can actually see a muscle delineation in my thighs and biceps!

"The trip to the health club for aerobics classes has become an absolute habit for me. I attend classes over lunch hour once or twice a week, if my evening schedule is hectic. And I will not miss the one and one-half hour Sunday morning workout. The Sunday workout is a gift to myself because I can take my time getting to the club and going home—no rushing involved. And that's a rare joy for me."

Mary wishes she could say that she enthusiastically looks forward to her workouts and that once she's there she's always energetic and enthused. But, the plain fact is, that's not the case. There are days she'd rather go home from work and relax over her lunch hour. She banishes those thoughts as quickly as she can so she doesn't cave in to them—and she rarely does. As previously stated, the trip to the club has become a habit. Why does she keep going if it occasionally feels like a chore? The hard news is that when she's been away from workouts for a week or two due to travel or vacation, she feels rotten. It's as simple as that. Her body feels somehow out of kilter, sluggish. She can feel the tension that's gathered in her muscles. It doesn't seem fair that this happens if she's away from aerobics for only a week, but it does. When she stops exercising, she notices what a difference the workout makes in how she feels physically and mentally. Being able to maintain the discipline of doing something that's good for her over an extended period of time is a real boost to her self-esteem.

Occasionally—depending on the aerobics instructor—there are also elements of dance incorporated into the aerobics routines. Having taken five years of ballet as a girl and two years of ballroom dancing as an adult, she really enjoys the moments of pure dance exercise. Doing a few Michael Jackson dance steps to "Bad" can't help but bring smiles to the faces of all ten or twelve participants in the Sunday morning class.

Another turning point in the lifetime weight battle for Mary was reading Sondra Ray's book, *The Only Diet There Is*. Ray's belief is that excess weight really is rooted in emotional issues. We have reasons why we eat—even though they may be deeply buried in the subconscious. Bringing some of these reasons to conscious awareness was a very powerful—and sometimes painful—process for Mary, but one which was also very liberating. Once she realized that her thought patterns had a great deal to do with causing excess weight, she could bring those thought patterns to conscious awareness. Then she could substitute healthier thought patterns using tools such as affirmations and creative visualization.

"I can't say I've attained my ideal weight, but I know I will. And, in the meantime, I'll be patient and gentle with myself. When I'm ready emotionally to let go of the last ten pounds I want to lose, I will. But I know I have to be emotionally ready to release that barrier.

"I realize that I've gained five pounds in the last eight weeks due to extra eating over anxiety and a schedule that hasn't permitted me to work out more than once or twice a week. Since my metabolism is used to a three-times-a-week workout, when that exercise pattern changes and I don't cut back on food, I know I'll gain several pounds. But since this has happened only two to three times over the past two years, I'm confident that once I settle back into a comfortable three-times-a-week workout pattern, I'll lose the pounds and feel better. I've learned to trust myself more and to be more patient with myself, and that has been a tremendous learning process as well."

Mary has made progress, but she knows there's more to be made. She has developed a discipline of exercise that is gratifying; she has lost some weight, developed muscles, and feels and looks better. Though she lost only ten to twelve pounds in the first six months of aerobics, all her clothes began to fit. She was certainly burning off fat, but since she was also increasing her muscle mass, the actual number of pounds she shed wasn't large. What was important to her during this phase was not what the dial on the scale told her, but what the mirror and the feel of her clothes told her. She could see the improved muscle tone; she could feel her clothes fitting better and feel the sense of accomplishment about doing good things for her inner body as well as her outer body.

Whatever form of exercise we choose, the mental and physical rewards of sticking to it are considerable. The weight and health benefits are important and can add years to our lives. But most importantly, the act of taking care of ourselves and loving ourselves enough to want what's good and healthy for our bodies is a positive mental lifestyle approach. And a positive mental approach to our lifestyle is a key element in our recovery.

CHAPTER TWENTY

IIIIIIIIIIIIIIIIIIIIIIIIIIIIIIIIIIIIIIIIIIIIIIIIIIIIIIIIIIIIIIIIIIIIIIIIIIIII

Understanding and Using Subliminal Techniques

Another approach that you might choose to explore is the use of subliminal techniques. Let's look at some examples of how subliminal learning works.

At a major university, an experiment tracked the impact of subliminal learning on foreign language students.[1] Thirty days prior to the first day of class, a limited number of students were played tapes as they slept, providing basic information about the language. Students in this group learned the language 80 to 90 percent faster than the students who had no such preparation.

Actors and actresses frequently record their lines on tape and listen to the tapes for faster memorization. Perhaps you've learned songs, rhymes, or commercials simply by being exposed to them frequently rather than by consciously listening to them. In subliminal learning, conscious listening is not necessary because information will automatically imprint on the subconscious mind.

How the Conscious and Subconscious Minds Work

To learn how we can use the power of the subconscious to benefit our lives, let's examine the functioning of the conscious and subconscious minds.

The Conscious Mind

The conscious mind absorbs information from the five senses—sight, sound, smell, taste, and touch. It is the part of our mind that makes choices and decisions. It is the conscious mind that urges us to take an umbrella if it looks like rain, to choose the shorter line at the bank, or to pick one brand of detergent over another. All information gathered by the conscious mind is stored in the subconscious mind for further reference.

The Subconscious Mind

The subconscious controls the *autonomic nervous system* of our heart, digestion, respiratory system, and other body functions. Although we don't consciously think about these functions, they occur with precision for many of us because of the functioning of the subconscious mind. Our heart beats and our blood flows; these processes become automatic for us, so we need not occupy our minds with them.

When we first learn to swim, we experience swimming at the conscious level. We find that we must think about each stroke and our head and leg movements. But within a short time, many of the swimming strokes, which at first were necessary to consciously think about, become automatic. The same is true for learning to bowl, learning the multiplication tables, or learning to dance.

The mind is like a great piece of literature. A small amount of its potential is available on the surface, just as a small amount of understanding is available on the first reading of an excellent short story. But beneath the surface of a short story are the symbolism, characterization, theme, and emotion. Similarly, beneath the conscious mind are the powerful components of the subconscious mind.

Empowering Ourselves Through the Subconscious

Several components of the subconscious mind are especially important for us to understand if we are to empower ourselves and create what we want in our lives.

It is the programming in your subconscious that produces your behaviors, actions, and reactions. For instance, let's say that as a fifth grader you missed a particular vault on the sidehorse and sprained your ankle. You may have consciously forgotten about this incident and the pain you felt. But you notice when you're twenty-six that you feel tense when you walk into a high school gymnasium one night and see a sidehorse. The memory, feelings, and impressions of this accident have been stored in your subconscious and are triggered by the sight of the sidehorse. Your sense of sight takes in the image of the sidehorse, and then your subconscious takes over by creating a physiological reaction based on the feelings surrounding the fifth grade accident. Your muscles tighten, and your breath becomes shallower. Your belief system, which was formed from your fifth grade experience, tells you: *watch out, sidehorses can be dangerous.* This subconscious thought produces the reality of your physiological sensations.

No matter what thoughts, feelings, or ideas the conscious mind imprints on the subconscious mind, the subconscious mind will creatively find a way to bring about such results. Take, for instance, the case of Belinda.

Belinda's Story

. . . as the six-month date approached, my subconscious automatically issued a "warning" to me.

"I had been through a series of relationships that had been quite painful," Belinda recalls. "I couldn't understand why the same pattern kept repeating in my life—especially when I didn't consciously want to repeat it. I now found myself with a man who was bright, caring, and kind. This relationship felt totally different from previous relationships: I didn't feel needy and lonely. Instead, I felt loved and cared about in a way that was totally new for me.

"About six months into the relationship, I started to feel anxious and tense. The unconscious tension created some distance between Ron and me. Soon we found ourselves edgy with each other and picking fights. I realized after long, hard thought that my previous relationships had usually lasted only six months. So as the six-month anniversary date of my relationship with Ron approached, my subconscious automatically issued a 'warning' to me. Although I wasn't consciously acting or talking any differently, I had unconsciously adopted a certain physiological tension and barrier that was certainly driving a wedge between Ron and me. The fear that this relationship would end after only six months—just as the other relationships had—did almost result in the end of my relationship with Ron. But luckily, I became aware of what I was doing. Once I became aware of what was going on subconsciously, I decided to get rid of my fear by becoming proactive in my fight against this negative thought pattern. I talked to friends, exercised more, wrote affirmations in my journal, and did my relaxation exercises in a much more consistent way. I was able to alter the subconscious, negative patterns in my mind by consciously creating new, healthy behaviors.''

Aha Experiences

The subconscious mind can also unleash creative solutions, ideas, and thoughts. Have you ever had a problem that you just couldn't seem to figure out? You probably examined it from many sides without arriving at a satisfactory solution. And then one morning you woke up and knew exactly what you needed to do to solve the problem. Your subconscious had been at work while you were asleep and had provided a solution for you.

Many of us have had this kind of mysterious, useful experience.

Several books have been written that document the prevalence of this experience among scientists and artists. Many great scientists, including American inventor Thomas Edison and Scottish inventor James Watt, have undergone such ''aha'' experiences. The subconscious selects its own timetable when understandings and insights pop into our conscious minds. Such events usually occur during a period of relaxation that follows a period of intense concentration on a problem. Walking in a park, showering, fishing, gardening, horseback riding, sailing, playing cards, gazing at the stars, lying on a dock in the July sun—these and other relaxing activities can be the fertile ground for an ''aha'' insight. In practically every case, such insights do not occur when we are dealing with our problems at a conscious level.

Goal-directed application of the subconscious has helped artists, scientists, inventors, athletes, and statesmen throughout history. It's helped them see new aspects of problems, visualize successful fulfillment of a purpose or activity, and gain additional motivation. It can work equally well for us.

Tapping the Subconscious Through Our Dreams

One of the ways we can access the power of the subconscious is through our dreams. Dreams are a powerful, subconscious resource that can assist us in a wide variety of ways. Dreams can help us to not only find creative solutions to problems, but to better understand our bodies, our hopes, our relationships, and our desires.

If you are having difficulty finding a solution to a problem, you may wish to use your dream process as a tool for guidance. Try focusing on a question related to your problem just before falling asleep. For instance, if you are wondering how to handle a certain situation at work, you may want to ask yourself, *What is the best way to handle the Tuesday meeting?* Repeat this question over and over as you drift off to sleep. You just may find when you awake the next morning that you know precisely how to lead the Tuesday meeting.

You may want to periodically review your dreams. Perhaps you'll notice recurring dreams or clearly see where and how you play certain of your dream roles in your life.

Our thoughts, feelings, and beliefs need to function together for us to achieve our goals. Without even consciously realizing it, we might think one thing, believe something else, and feel a third thing. What we truly, deeply believe produces the thoughts that can result in changes in our life. But for changes to occur, we must change our thinking and beliefs. This is not always easy, since most of us spend more time thinking about what we don't want rather than what we do want. It's essential that our thinking be geared toward what we do want.

Baby elephants are frequently kept from roaming off by putting a rope loosely around their necks and attaching that rope to a stake in the ground. When a baby elephant raised in this way grows up, it can still be kept from roaming off by using this same method. Even though the grown elephant weighs thousands of pounds and could easily pull the stake from the ground, it is conditioned by past experience to believe that it can't get away.

Humans function in a similar way. Our deeply held thoughts and beliefs directly impact our actions. Changing our thinking and beliefs at the conscious level frees our subconscious to harness these new thoughts and beliefs and produce results that align with them. Hence, our subconscious storehouse of power and creativity can be directed by our conscious mind. But for this creative energy to produce results desired by each of us, our subconscious can and must be consciously and purposefully directed. Saying affirmations, visualizing, and setting goals are some conscious techniques and tools that can be used to induce the incredible power of the subconscious in our daily lives. In the chapters that follow, we'll discuss these and other techniques in detail.

CHAPTER TWENTY-ONE

||||||||||||||||||||||||||||||||||||||||||||||||||||||||||||||||||||||||||||||||

Using Relaxation Exercises, Guided Imagery, and Meditation

The word *meditation* may sound esoteric and exotic. But the fact is, many people take time each day to visualize their goals and dreams through guided imagery and meditation. This helps them in several important ways. First, they focus energy on their goals, creating greater expectations and hope in their life. Second, visualizing their life as they wish it to be creates a sense of joy, happiness, and positive expectancy. Third, it can help to start their day on an upbeat note that carries into all their activities.

People also experience distinct physiological benefits when they use these techniques. Let's look at the basics of what happens to the body when it relaxes.

The Benefits of Relaxation

When in a relaxed state, your brain waves shift from the normal, alert beta rhythm to the relaxed alpha rhythm. Your breathing rate slows and oxygen consumption decreases. Your heart rate and blood pressure drop, and the blood flow to your muscles decreases. An overall reduction in the metabolism occurs. Blood flow is directed to your brain and skin, producing a feeling of warmth and rested mental alertness. Relaxation enables us to quiet the mind and rejuvenate the body. These changes counteract the harmful and uncomfortable effects of stress in our bodies.

Anxiety and Stress Reduction

Anxiety or stress produces the hormones adrenaline and noradrenaline. When these substances are produced frequently, they can cause, or be a strong contributing factor in, many illnesses, including hypertension, backaches, tension headaches, muscle aches, insomnia, and cardiac rhythm disturbances.

Our ancestors were able to take the physical action necessary to dissipate these hormones—the so-called *fight or flight response*. But in today's society, most of us face more emotional stress than physical stress. Though we are unlikely to need to activate the fight or flight response because we've encountered a saber-toothed tiger on our way to work, we are likely to encounter a metaphorical "saber-toothed tiger" in the form of our boss, a client, or a project deadline. As the stress- and anxiety-producing substances are activated, for emotional rather than physical stresses, they "attack" the body rather than enable the body to contend with dangerous outside factors. By blocking the action of the hormones adrenaline and noradrenaline, relaxation reduces anxiety and other harmful effects that are a response to the fight or flight reaction.

Interrupting Negative Thought Patterns

Another very powerful benefit of using relaxation techniques is the interruption and short-circuiting of harmful, negative thought patterns. Have you ever been unable to sleep because your mind is racing and generating more anxiety as you keep going over the same negative thoughts? This vicious cycle raises anxiety levels and results in no concrete solutions, choices, or action plans. Interrupting the cycle of these thoughts will reduce anxiety and frequently clear the mind so a creative solution to the problem can be found.

Interrupting the anxiety cycle also reduces fear and can result in the development of more positive expectations. Developing more positive expectations further reduces fear. It's better to have this positive snowball cycle than the anxiety and fear cycle previously described.

Feeling a Sense of Control in Our Life

In addition to short-circuiting negative thought patterns and reducing anxiety and tension, practicing relaxation techniques also enhances our sense of confidence that we do have some control of our body, feelings, and thoughts. In numerous research studies outlined in Blair Justice's book, *Who Gets Sick*, the concept of having some control in our life is an extremely important, life-enhancing factor.

As you feel and react in healthy ways, your overall sense of self-esteem is enhanced. You lose more and more fear as you learn that you can create choices, both physiologically and mentally, through relaxation. Relaxation also allows you to draw on your intuition and creativity to assist you in moving in the direction that's important for you.

Anxiety-related symptoms such as constipation, diarrhea, vomiting, nausea, and having a short temper can be reduced or eliminated through relaxation exercises. Jan personally found a way to deal with the problem of her short temper.

Jan's Story
Taking a "Mental Vacation"

"On the rare occasions when I'm not able to take twenty minutes for relaxation in the morning, I feel more 'on edge' or slightly anxious," Jan says. "I'm far more likely to feel tension. This produces panic when I encounter a problem at work. Rather than relaxing and taking a creative problem-solving approach, I become more tense. Such anxiety responses tend to inhibit my productivity. And that, in turn, can produce more anxiety.

"If I find myself in the middle of such a pattern, I'll try to take a five-minute *mental vacation*. I'll close my eyes, sit as comfortably as possible, breathe deeply, and picture myself in my favorite place. I'll hear the sounds of water lapping against the shore, smell the fragrance of flowers, and feel the sun on my skin. I'll hear the rustle of the breeze in the trees and smell the soft scent of pine as I relax on my beach towel.

"By engaging as many senses as I can in this process of imaging my ideal vacation scene, I make it as 'real' as possible and experience the relaxation mentally. This mental imagery is a stress break that works."

If we meditate or use relaxation exercises regularly, we will begin to realize that our strong emotions, which used to cause us great pain and anxiety, no longer have the same impact. We will still feel anger, resentment, and fear—let's face it, we are still human beings—but the grip of these emotions won't be as powerful. Meditation and relaxation focus our attention on higher awareness. In this process we nurture and release our intuition and creativity. When this happens, we find ourselves more willing to experience new activities, take more risks, and focus on what "can be" instead of "what could have been." We release negative thought patterns that once held us back, and we direct our attention to the positive here and now.

Relaxation and Meditation Techniques

A number of excellent books on relaxation and meditation techniques are listed in the Select Bibliography. In the section that follows, we've listed some ideas and techniques you may wish to consider as you begin exploring this process. Please be aware that what works for one person may not be the most appropriate technique for you. Try a variety of approaches or techniques until you find one that feels right and is comfortable for you.

One woman was convinced of the benefits of meditation and tried several approaches that friends recommended over a period of several years. But she felt that she hadn't found what worked for her. Finally, during a plane ride to a conference, she accidentally experienced a process that worked for her. She created a picture in her mind of a black sky dotted with sparkling stars and repeated the word *peace* to herself. So, be willing to experiment until you find a process that fits you.

The very first time you try relaxation or meditation techniques, you may not be convinced of the necessity of this process in your daily life. Some of us may immediately experience the rewards of this activity, but for many of us, it will take a few weeks or months to learn to quiet the chattering mind and let go. Be patient with yourself as you discover what works for you, realizing that each day you practice relaxation and meditation exercises will provide further gifts for your body and mind.

Just as in exercising, you may not fully appreciate the beneficial effects on your mind and body as you relax or meditate until you miss a few days. Then, your body and mind will let you know that your "neglect" is not appreciated!

Please also realize that your experiences each day will vary. On some days, you will slip into relaxation or meditation with astounding ease; on other days, your mind and body will fight you every step of the way. This variation is certainly natural. Don't fight it; just accept it.

Listening to Relaxation Tapes

You may first wish to listen to relaxation tapes. Tapes can guide you into the process in an easy, pleasant manner. You may want to check with friends to see if anyone has tapes you might borrow. Or consider checking out tapes from your local library so you can find one you like before spending money. You might prefer guided imagery tapes that provide initial relaxation instructions and then gradually guide you into a relaxing journey. Or perhaps once you're comfortable with a particular relaxation routine, you can listen to a tape of beautiful, floating music that will provide a soft, gentle background as you relax your body and slip into a peaceful, meditative state.

Joe, for example, likes to use a tape that guides him through an initial relaxation process and then provides peaceful music. Since this was such a powerful tape for him, he used it with a class he was teaching and had an interesting response. Several of the students were trained as pianists, and they found the solo piano music, which Joe found so peaceful, to be very distracting. Because of their piano training, they tended to "play" the music as they listened to the tape rather than relax. So, the process is different for everyone.

Meditating

Perhaps you'll wish to try the more traditional approaches of meditation that involve meditating on a particular spiritual concept such as love, peace, or light, or repeating a word or phrase over and over. Whatever method you choose, be sure to find a quiet, peaceful place where you can be alone for ten to fifteen minutes without interruption.

Many people heartily recommend meditating or practicing relaxation techniques first thing in the morning since it helps them establish a positive tone for the day. But again, pay attention to your own needs and establish a time that fits into your rhythm and lifestyle. Give yourself a trial period of at least a month. It takes twenty-one days to firmly establish a new habit, and once relaxation or meditation becomes a habit, it will be natural for you to include it in your day. Just as not brushing your teeth in the morning may feel awkward, missing daily meditation will most likely produce the same kind of reaction once it becomes an established pattern in your life.

Just as in any change we undergo, we will most likely experience some initial resistance to the meditation or relaxation process. This is to be expected. Often we'll start a project, try it for a while, and then drop it when we don't immediately get results.

If you try for a while and don't feel you're making progress, you may want to vary your technique, read more on the subject, or try a meditation class. Or, you may want to attend a workshop, or talk to an instructor who might provide encouragement or recommend other techniques. Moving beyond the initial resistance requires commitment to overcome the frustrations, fears, and doubts that might be raised along the way. Remember, the process is a powerful gift: it shows you are committed to loving and nurturing yourself regularly.

CHAPTER TWENTY-TWO

‖‖‖

Incorporating Visualization Techniques into Your Life

Another very positive tool that you may wish to investigate is visualization. It's a natural, powerful ability that each of us has. It is a tool that each of us can use to create more choices in our life. Let's examine how it works.

You may have one or more special places—places that for a variety of reasons create a unique and compelling emotional attachment for you. These places may bring a smile to your face and produce a feeling of joy, peace, and serenity. It may be a park five minutes from your home or a spot halfway around the world.

When we think of these places, we automatically picture them in our mind. And usually without even realizing it, these locations trigger a variety of sensory responses, which is another reason they have such a powerful, emotional impact for us. We smell pine or salt water or a crackling fire; we hear a particular bird's song or the sound of children playing; we feel the hot, sun-warmed sand caressing our toes, or the cool breeze against our face.

Think about a special location and feel what sensory images surface for you. Can you not only *see* the spot, but also *hear* sounds you associate with it and *smell* its unique smells?

Visualizing events, actions, or places is a natural and automatic process that you perform each day. For instance, if you hear the word *Tootsie Roll*, do you picture the wrapper, smell and taste the Tootsie Roll, feel the texture as you chew it? If you are extremely hungry and on the way to your relatives' house for Thanksgiving dinner, do you smell the turkey and dressing, see the rich color, and taste the pumpkin pie? And this visualization process doesn't just happen with food. If we think about going fishing, shopping for wallpaper, or dashing into the bank, we form automatic mental images of the locations and our actions.

The Benefits of Visualization

Since we use *visualization* constantly and naturally, why not use it in a purposeful, creative way to help us realize our dreams and goals? What we expect, believe, and picture we usually get. For many of us adult children, what we expect, believe, and picture has been negative. At some deep level, we don't expect our relationships to succeed. *Normal* to us may mean not getting our needs met. To change some of these negative patterns and habits, let's direct this powerful, positive tool of visualization toward maximizing our potential and getting what we want.

The conscious mind can decide what it wants to think and what it wants to achieve, but the subconscious mind is the servant of the conscious mind. It receives and works toward using the information presented by the conscious mind. So if a very conscious effort is made to visualize positive results, the subconscious will be an ally in this process. Remember, the subconscious mind does not know the difference between an image in your mind and an actual image, for instance, a picture on the wall of your living room.

To verify this, close your eyes and vividly imagine a lemon. Picture the rough, textured, yellow surface of the lemon. Now imagine picking up a white plate—one so shiny that you can see your reflection in it. Place the lemon on the plate, pick up a serrated knife and cut the lemon in half. Feel the lemon juice trickling down your fingers. Then cut the lemon in quarters and smell the tangy aroma of the lemon. Watch the juice trickling down the side of the lemon as you put down the knife.

Now pick up one of the lemon quarters. Feel the rough texture, smell the lemon smell, and bring it slowly to your mouth. Now bite into the lemon.

Did your mouth pucker? Did your throat react as though you had a real lemon in your hand that you were about to bite into? For most people, the answer is yes. Even though you didn't have a real lemon, the vivid picture in your mind produced a physiological reaction similar to the reaction you would have had with an actual lemon.

Bill's Story
Learning to Type While Being Motionless

James W. Newman in his book, *Release Your Brakes!* provides two dramatic examples of the power of visualization to bring about results.[1] After having surgery to remove shrapnel from his back, a young soldier, named Bill, was required to lie motionless for weeks in a hospital bed or he would be paralyzed. He watched TV, listened to the radio, and read by having a nurse put a magazine or book in a rack over his bed.

As time wore on, he thought about the fact that he'd always wanted to learn to type. He decided this was an ideal time to study and memorize the typewriter keyboard. One of the nurses found a typing text in the hospital library. First, he memorized the keyboard and fingering system. Then, he closed his eyes and imagined his fingers on a keyboard and he'd see the letters and sentences that he typed on paper. He'd "practice" typing for fifteen to twenty minutes at a time.

After completing an intensive physical therapy program, he walked into the hospital office and asked if he could use a typewriter. In his first attempt to actually type, he typed fifty-five error-free words a minute.

Prisoners of war in Vietnam frequently found ways to keep their minds occupied during solitary confinement. One Air Force officer who was an excellent golfer practiced eighteen holes in his mind every day during all seven years of his confinement. In spite of seven years without actually playing golf, he shot par when he played his first round after returning home.[2]

Perhaps you've practiced the fingering of a musical instrument in your mind or learned shorthand through this process. Visualizing does produce results.

Visualization Means Being There—Totally

One of the most important concepts of visualization is to *experience* the visualization rather than just observe it. That means placing yourself into the heart of the action, not just watching it. The more vividly experienced, the more deeply embedded the image will be in the subconscious. Therefore, use as many of your senses as possible as you picture your goal.

If, for instance, you are visualizing the San Francisco vacation you're saving for, you might picture yourself getting off the plane at the San Francisco airport, feeling the balmy temperature, smelling the breeze from the bay, hearing the clang of the trolley cars, tasting the fresh scallops, and feeling the sand under your toes as you walk along a beach.

It's also important to picture what you want to happen as if it has already happened or is already happening. This allows you to create an inner experience of how it feels to have your desire or goal realized.

Some Important Things to Remember

As in anything else, it's important to practice and use this tool consistently. You might find that the very best time to practice is just before falling asleep or just after waking. As you relax before falling asleep or as you gradually awaken, you are more susceptible to suggestion—you are less likely to be analytical and question the process.

Be Gentle on Yourself and Let Your Patience Shine Through:
Don't Force Change

Realize, however, that *forcing* change with imaginative mind action is usually counterproductive. To fully realize this powerful tool of visualization effectively, we will need to *allow* change to occur. When we try forcing our will due to fear or doubt, we only succeed in reinforcing the fear and doubt.

Since most of us are used to gritting our teeth, rolling up our sleeves, and tackling things with sheer force, it's not easy for us to allow change rather than force it. Most of us are looking for immediate results.

As Newman points out, lasting behavior changes resemble the process of an ocean liner changing course.[3] As the ship turns, it also continues to move forward in the direction it has been going. So, too, some of your old behavior patterns will stay with you for a while. This is natural and to be expected. Remember that this is a process and not an immediate occurrence. So expect gradual rather than instant results. They will occur, but allow yourself time and be gentle on yourself.

SPECIFIC VISUALIZATION TECHNIQUES

There is no right or wrong method; there is only the method that works best for you.

- *The first step is to pick a goal.* Pick as your starting goal the one for which you feel the most emotion and passion. It could be, *I want to lose ten pounds,* or *I want to be more assertive in my personal life.*
- *Next, turn your goal into a positive affirmation.* Combining affirmations with visualization is an especially powerful tool because the verbal affirmation can combine with the conceptual and emotional elements of visualization. For instance, the weight goal for a 150-pound woman who wants to lose 10 pounds could become the affirmation, *I weigh 140 pounds.* The assertiveness goal could become the affirmation, *I am an assertive person.*
- *Picture or feel this affirmation.* See yourself at a party or at the beach. You weigh your ideal weight. Picture yourself being assertive in a special situation with your best friend or your boss. Use as many senses as you can to experience yourself being assertive, and let yourself feel very good and positive about the outcome.
- *Relax and allow the changes to occur rather than forcing them.* Sometimes they may not be on the timetable that you'd most want, but be assured that they are on the timetable that is best for you.

If you doubt the truth of your affirmation, remember that when you visualize and affirm your goal *it does exist as an idea.* Nothing can ever be created without first being conceived as an idea. Once the idea is born, it is powerful and can take on a life of its own. If you feel strongly enough about your goal, your energy and positive belief will allow it to happen.

Practicing Visualization

When you first practice visualization, remember that there is no simple right way. You may simply sense or feel images rather than picture them in detail in your mind. That's fine.

Also, it's usually a good idea to visualize one goal at a time. It's easier to bring all your senses into play when you focus your energy on one particular goal. You may want to take ten minutes when you first wake up to visualize your goal, and spend another ten minutes doing the same thing before you fall asleep at night. You may also want to write out your goal as an affirmation at some point during the day.

The important thing is to find a method that works best for you. Perhaps early morning is your peak period for visualization. Starting the day in such a manner will be beneficial for your outlook that day and may put you in a positive frame of mind to meet the tasks ahead. Or if you are a night person, the time just before falling asleep may be the best time to review your goal. If your goal is the last thought on your mind before falling asleep, you have a strong opportunity to put your conscious thought into the subconscious.

Relax and visualize an ideal scene of your goal as reality. See your achievement, hear it, smell it, taste it, live it, celebrate it, and feel the joy of it in your body.

Visualization can be pictures, words (affirmations), and images. It can be used to help you reach your goals in any aspect of your life. It is a natural process, one you do automatically every day, and one that can become extremely powerful through practice. It is, most of all, an exciting process of using your imagination to create what you want in your life.

CHAPTER TWENTY-THREE

||||||||||||||||||||||||||||||||||||||||||||||||||||||||||||||||||||||||

Using Affirmations to Break Old Patterns

Another method closely related to visualization is the use of affirmations. In this chapter we'll explore how this process works.

Have you ever noticed, in a quiet moment, just how many messages, thoughts, feelings, and impressions are running through your mind? You might be noticing the cold draft on your feet; the desire for more coffee; the need to send that birthday card off to your sister-in-law; the note to pick up the dry cleaning on the way home from work; the necessity of finishing that report for your boss today; or the need to call your friend about cancelling your lunch appointment for next week. All of these thoughts, feelings, and images have traveled through your mind in a second or two, and you may think there appears to be no end in sight to the thoughts coming through.

Our minds can be forceful, creative, memorable tools that keep us on course and on time. But for most of us, sifting through the incredible number of bits of information is an impossible task until we can shut off or slow down the "noise." And sometimes when we are depressed or discouraged, the "noise" becomes a negative cycle of thoughts and we get stuck in this negative cycle.

Janel's Story

> . . . *the sound of my voice very definitely changed as I read*
> *through the affirmations.*

Janel was sitting on her bed feeling very discouraged. It was clear to her that she had focused her affections on someone who could not reciprocate.

"After wallowing in self-pity for a few hours, I decided to try a technique I'd been reading about—affirmations. I'd read about the power of affirmations and had even written out a few of them for myself. Occasionally I'd read them over, but never consistently. But now I decided to try something I'd recently read about—recording my affirmations on tape. Besides, I figured that if nothing else, just forging ahead on a project of *any* kind would probably serve to get my mind off its present negative track.

"I found an old, used audiotape and decided to record over it. I looked over the sheets of paper and four-by-six-inch note cards on which I'd jotted down a number of affirmations, and I checked off the ones that I liked the best. I decided to record affirmations that dealt with all areas of my life—health, finances, career, relationships, my sense of self. I read the affirmations into my tape recorder, then repeated this process several more times until I had a tape that was about twenty minutes long."

Janel then played the tape back. She was stunned. "As I listened I realized that the sound of my voice very definitely changed as I read through the affirmations. My voice sounded flat and lifeless as I read the first four or five affirmations, but sounded far more upbeat as I went on. There were traces of confidence and enthusiasm. I could actually hear myself feeling better as I kept recording the affirmations.

"I couldn't dispute what my own ears had heard. The affirmations *did* change my attitude and therefore actually changed the sound of my voice. I was truly astonished."

Shortly after her discovery, Janel came across a magazine article about Susan Jeffers, author of the book, *Feel the Fear and Do It Anyway.*[1] According to the article, Jeffers used a technique in her seminars that never failed to astonish the participants. She'd ask for a volunteer from the audience, and when the volunteer came to the front of the room, she'd ask the volunteer to hold her arm out straight in front of her. When Jeffers said ''go,'' she would try to push the volunteer's arm down, and the volunteer would try to resist. In all cases, the volunteer was able to resist this effort to push her arm down. Next, Jeffers asked the volunteer to repeat out loud ten times the phrase, ''I am a weak and unworthy person.'' Then Jeffers asked the volunteer to repeat the previous exercise of resisting as Jeffers tried to push her arm down. This time, however, Jeffers was able to effortlessly push the volunteer's arm down. According to Jeffers, it never failed.

Although Janel was firmly convinced of the power of affirmations after her experience of reading affirmations into her tape recorder, a part of her was still skeptical about Jeffers' findings. So, she decided to check it out for herself. ''First I tried it with a couple of my friends. To their astonishment and to mine, it worked exactly as Susan Jeffers indicated it would. After my friend repeated the phrase, 'I am a weak and unworthy person,' I was always able to push her arm down.''

What We Desire Is Already in Our Lives

In Chapter Twenty-One, we learned how, through relaxation exercises and meditation, to hold one thought at a time. Here we're talking about purposefully introducing and using certain thoughts and images in our mind through the use of affirmations. In some cases, this means changing the nature of our self-talk from the negative *I never mail birthday cards on time— I sure am inconsiderate, selfish, and unorganized* to the positive *I am an efficient, organized person—I always have time to do what I really want.*

In *Creative Visualization*, Shakti Gawain describes an *affirmation* as a strong, positive statement that something is already so. The purpose for using affirmations is not only to change the unconscious negative noise that we make inside our heads. It's also to purposefully and consciously acknowledge that what we desire is already so in our life.

For example, if you are trying to quit smoking, an affirmation that would be useful is: *I* (your name) *am a nonsmoker*. If you use this affirmation every day, you could eventually re-program your inner voice that is presently saying things such as: *I'll never be able to quit. . . . I can't quit; I know because I've tried five times. . . . I can't quit; I'll gain a lot of weight. . . . I can't quit; I'll get too crabby.* Using a positive affirmation every day (*I* [your name] *am a nonsmoker*) will imprint on your subconscious the new message of you as a nonsmoker.

Tips on Using Affirmations

Affirmations can be

- written,
- spoken out loud,
- spoken to yourself, and
- put on tape and listened to.

You may want to use all four methods during the same time period because, in that way, you'll engage more of your senses and ultimately more of your conscious mind.

Many people also occasionally tape a particularly important affirmation to their bathroom mirror so it is one of the first things they see in the morning. That way, they start their self-talk off with positive, healthy thoughts.

Be Positive

As mentioned earlier, affirmations are positive statements, so when you are constructing yours, make sure you are asking for what you do want:

   I (your name) *am a nonsmoker.*
NOT
I (your name) *don't smoke anymore.*

The word *nonsmoker* becomes a part of your identity this way, and the subconscious will be reprogrammed to fulfill this new aspect of yourself. ''Don't smoke anymore'' is a negative statement, and your subconscious won't respond as well or as quickly to negative messages even if you intend a positive outcome.

Three Forms of Affirmations

When you are writing out your affirmations, it's helpful to write them in first, second, and third person:

First person: *I* (name) *am a nonsmoker.*
Second person: *You* (name) *are a nonsmoker.*
Third person: *She* (name) *is a nonsmoker.*

Write each form of the affirmation twenty or thirty times a day, and then move on to the next form until you have written all three. Using these three forms is also helpful when you are speaking them out loud to yourself or taping them.

If you have a friend you trust and whose voice you enjoy listening to, you may ask that person to record some of your affirmations. It is sometimes easier to pay attention to a friend's voice, and it can be a pleasant change of pace for you.

FINDING THE RIGHT AFFIRMATIONS

You may be asking yourself, *Where can I find inspiration for writing the kinds of affirmations that would be most useful to me?* In Chapter Four (pages 48–55), you learned about goal setting. Review the goals that you have written down and choose the area that is most important to you currently; this might be goals in relationships, spiritual and personal growth, career, or finances. In that area, choose just one goal to work with. For example, under financial goals you may have listed five or six goals, both short- and long-term. Your short-term goal list may look something like this:

Short-Term Goals
1. Pay off credit card bill of $800 by December 21.
2. Save $125 each month for one year.
3. Secure midyear raise of $2,800.
4. Carry bag lunch three times each week and put money saved toward cost of new watch ($150): $5 per lunch saved, $15 per week for ten weeks.
5. Check out loan rate at five banks. What do they charge for new car loans?

Of these goals, the hardest one for you to continue may be saving $125 each month. It may seem hard to save that money and not buy that new suit or those home furnishings that you've had your eye on. You may feel deprived by putting the money in the bank and not having as much to spend on personal, fun items. Affirmations that might be useful here include:

- *I* (your name) *feel really good about saving money.*
- *I* (your name) *enjoy saving money.*
- *I* (your name) *enjoy saving $125 each month.*
- *I* (your name) *experience financial abundance in my life every day.*
- *I* (your name) *am healthy, happy, and prosperous.*

Please remember that these are examples. If you have an inspiration, please use it. The more personal your affirmations are, the more they'll speak directly to the situation in language you enjoy, and the faster they'll work.

How the Negative Can Reach the Positive

If you still feel stumped, try phrasing the situation in the negative. When you have the phrase down on paper, it might be easier to see how to make it into a positive statement. Brainstorm with it, going from Step A (the idea) to Step C (the affirmation) as follows:

A. Boy, I feel deprived not being able to buy that *(dress, suit, baseball glove, vase, whatever)*. If only I could spend the money I save. If I spend the money I save, I'll feel *(poor, awful, deprived, down, grumpy)*.
B. *I* want to feel good about what I'm doing.
C. *I (your name)* feel good about saving $125 each month.

Some people write the first part of the affirmation in the negative and end it with a positive phrase:

I (name) *don't feel deprived when I save money. I experience financial abundance in my life every day.*

If you wish to start with a negative phrase to help clarify the situation, always end it with a positive phrase. Many people find that after phrasing their affirmations in the negative, the positive affirmation just kind of pops out at them. Some situations don't seem to lend themselves to only a positive phrase, so use the *negative-positive technique* if you wish.

It's important to use affirmations every day, and it's important that you focus them on one or two goals at a time. Don't try and keep ten or fifteen affirmations going; it's confusing and can dilute the purpose. Choose one or two areas of your life that are important, and use one or two affirmations for each goal or area. You can really concentrate your energy this way and keep your mind from wandering off.

The rhythm of an affirmation can be important. Many people choose their affirmations on the weekend and then use them all week. Sometimes they will use four or five different affirmations during the week, but they'll all focus on only one topic. Sometimes when they have four or five to choose from, they'll find one that is really nice and stay with it the following week as well. Take time to be creative and experiment a little. If you do, you will enjoy the time you spend reprogramming your subconscious.

CHAPTER TWENTY-FOUR

||||||||||||||||||||||||||||||||||||||||||||||||||||||||||||||||||||||||

Journaling as a Tool for Release and Discovery

Perhaps at one time you kept a diary or a journal. Journaling is another positive recovery technique that just might fit for you.

Journaling is a process of recording thoughts, feelings, observations, desires, wishes, dreams, needs, or goals—whatever you feel is important to you—and organizing these "messages" in a useful way. It is somewhat like keeping a diary, yet it is broader than simply recording daily thoughts.

You can collect and organize these messages in three-ring binders, blank books, lined diaries with dated pages, folders, portfolios—whatever works for you is fine.

A journal can become an important way of gaining perspective on one's life, as Joel discovered.

Joel's Story
The practice of writing in a journal gave me something much more valuable than fortune or fame.

Joel began journaling as a high school sophomore because of an assignment from his English teacher. Joel says journaling has given him a record of the highs and lows of his life.

"Over the years, I've recorded many events in my life. This record has proven to be very useful to me ten and fifteen years later. I can find some of the happiest, saddest, most ordinary, inspiring, hopeful, challenging, and difficult events that have

happened to me and 're-live' them. This gives me a chance to
see these events in a different light, to see the changes I have
been able to make over time. And it helps me to validate, for
myself only, some difficult family events that have not been
openly discussed to this day.

"I am able to remember that it was hard to break up with
my college sweetheart and to remind myself that the decision
led to other beneficial events. I am able to put perspective on
the time that my former boss reprimanded me for not doing
my best work, and I can now see that I have indeed improved
my work habits. And I enjoyed greater satisfaction and success
because of the changes he had suggested. As an adult child I
often have trouble taking credit for good things I've done, seeing the benefits of changing my behaviors or attitudes, or being
willing to take risks to pursue goals. Journaling can help me
in all three of these areas."

Many people find that reading their journals reminds them
directly of the actions they have taken and the consequences.
Their record keeping also helps them see what methods have
been successful in helping them pursue change, such as visualization, affirmations, or meditation.

Journaling Can Be a Wide-Open, Creative Process

Sometimes you can record in writing your thoughts and feelings; sometimes you can draw the images that your feelings
evoke in you.

You can take magazines and cut out pictures that are perti-
nent to a goal you're pursuing or a visualization or affirmation
that you're using.

You can collect postcards and include them in your journal.

You can cut out job descriptions from the newspaper, or you
can paste in brochures that describe seminars that may interest
you.

Or you can undertake some flight of fancy or whimsy such
as describing your "perfect day."

If you would like to try an activity that sounds fun or whimsical, try writing it out in your journal and write yourself into the scene. It might be a way for you to practice what is, in effect, a different kind of visualization process. This process might open up your ability to visualize things internally in a more complete or satisfying way.

WHY KEEP A JOURNAL?

The reasons for keeping a journal vary from person to person and journal to journal.

- Many people keep journals to document their journey through life, work out confusing or overwhelming feelings, record snappy comebacks to previous conversations, or review fights with significant others.
- Journals are a great place to vent anger with no damage done or hurt given. When you've vented anger in your journal, you might have an easier time going back to the person you're having trouble with and resolving the situation.
- Journals are a good place to record the progress you are making toward a goal. It can be a "measuring device" to show yourself how far you've come and how far you may still be from where you would like to end up.

Joel's Story Continued
When I read my journals months later, I see that I have indeed reached my goals.

"I am an impatient person," Joel says, "and have often missed the progress I've made because I have been so busy berating myself for not being further along. When I read my journals months later, I see that I have indeed reached my goals and not taken credit and congratulated myself on staying with it. My journals help me be more realistic with the time lines I set and more compassionate with who I am now.

"I have also used journals at certain times to record dreams that I remember and to record some of the intuitive flashes I've had. Since I'm interested in learning to listen to myself better and find out what I need, recording these inner ideas and messages helps me validate them or release them later. By then, I've had sufficient time to understand what's valuable to me and what isn't.

"I try and keep an open mind and not have a lot of 'rules' anymore about my journaling process. Two rules that I do have are to, one, date each entry, and, two, not to throw out anything that I've written or drawn. Though I sometimes get frustrated because I don't think something is good enough, I often find that when I see something later, I see its merits more clearly."

If you think you might need some structure, try setting *time goals*, such as journaling for ten minutes each day or every other day for a month. Once you begin, you'll probably discover how much time you need or want for journaling, and how often you wish to do it. However you approach a journal, remember that your goal is to learn about yourself. You are the person most capable of knowing yourself. That is a magnificent goal and not easily attainable or comfortable. But if you live one day at a time, and take the time to occasionally record your experiences, a journal can help you track your progress.

Try keeping a journal for six months. Experiment with how often you write in it and what you add, if anything, in the way of photos or newspaper clippings. Play with the formats you use. Maybe try a folder and a three-ring binder. Or try a three-ring binder and a book with blank pages. Let your inner voice be your guide and have some fun. You may come to enjoy journaling, and it can be useful to you in learning more about yourself and how you grow.

PART FOUR

Recovery at Work

CHAPTER TWENTY-FIVE

Adult Children in
the Workplace

How do you usually feel on your day off when you remember that you have to work the next day? Are you pleased, excited, happy, and looking forward to returning? Are you indifferent or bored by the thought? Are you upset or anxious when thinking about returning to work? Perhaps what makes work so intriguing and important are the feelings it evokes in us. Few things are as personal except perhaps relationships and spirituality. And whether we work in our home, outside of it, or both, it occupies much of our time and energy. A close look at ourselves as workers and the dynamics of our workplaces can help us understand how our work affects our well-being.

For many of us, what pushed us to begin recovery was the pain we felt in our relationships. We had trouble relating with our parents, spouses, children, friends, and co-workers. Once in recovery, we found ways to begin to heal ourselves and important relationships. Sometimes we had to choose to leave a relationship, or maybe we moved toward new relationships with others. At other times we found greater joy than we thought possible in dealing in healthy ways with the alcoholics in our lives. We noticed and deeply felt our improvements and looked forward to continuing to get better.

Relating to our co-workers isn't significantly different than relating to other people—or is it? Let's examine some of the dynamics of the workplace and see how they can affect our sense of ourselves and our relationships with supervisors, co-workers, or those who work for us.

Say you're a bartender in a restaurant . . .

You like the work, the social camaraderie, and the people you work with, and don't mind the hours. One night, one of your regular customers has obviously had too much to drink, you believe. She asks for another drink, which you deny her. She gets up, stomps over to your boss, gives him an earful of what a nasty jerk you are, and leaves. Your boss comes over and asks what happened. You explain that she appeared intoxicated and so you wouldn't serve her anything more. Your boss tells you that your job is bartending, not offending the customers. He appears to give you the cold shoulder for the rest of the week. *What do you do?*

Say you're working as an apprentice carpenter . . .

Union positions in your town are *very* hard to come by, and you are determined to work as hard as you can, do your best work, and try to make the boss look good. You've got big dreams of someday being a general contractor, and you know that this job is a large part of your ticket to future success. After several months of ten-hour days and six-day work-weeks, you are finally invited out after work with the crew, a symbol of acceptance. While there, your boss tells you that he's having problems with one of the other apprentices, a good friend of yours, and asks for your advice. *What do you do?*

Say you're the young superstar salesperson in your company . . .

You work with a tightly knit group of other up-and-comers. You love your work, and you know that you are on the fast track to the top. Your immediate supervisor is transferred to another division, and her boss selects you as the person he believes is the best replacement. You walk out of his office and share your elation and success with one of your co-workers. In the next week you notice that none of the team includes you in the morning coffee klatches in the cafeteria, and no one stops by your desk to chat spontaneously. You feel as if you suddenly developed leprosy by achieving your dream. *What do you do?*

All of these scenarios are real. All of them were experienced by adult children, and none of them turned out the way the participants would have wished. None of them was easy to cope with. Yet they are mentioned time and again by Tim (the bartender), Cory (the carpenter), and Ellen (the new sales supervisor) as valuable incidents that contributed greatly to their personal growth. Let's examine each incident closely.

Tim's Story

The night I denied the drink to a regular customer appeared no different than many others.

Tim had been a bartender for three years. Starting in the same restaurant as a busboy, he had worked his way up to head bartender and night manager. Tim had drifted after high school working as a cook, a bus driver, construction worker, and even as a sanitation engineer, before he landed the restaurant job.

Though he knew bartending wasn't the best job for him given his childhood experience, he had long ago made peace with himself about his choice of profession. He really liked his work and felt proud of his progress in settling down into working regularly and being more responsible.

Tim's boss, Pat, owned the bar and restaurant. Pat was always kind and encouraging to Tim, especially because Tim was a hard worker who always gave a bit extra when asked. Over time, the two became friends even though Pat was fifteen years older than Tim. For the first time in his life, Tim felt that he was getting somewhere and that he was working for someone who was willing to give him a break.

Tim had started a recovery program about a year before the incident with the intoxicated customer had occurred. He regularly attended an adult children's meeting, and he had read several self-help and personal growth books. He found the meetings and books enlightening. Through his new friends, he'd begun to see himself as a likable and responsible person.

"The night I denied the drink to a regular customer appeared no different than many others. I had begun to create a new value system that supported not serving intoxicated customers. There were laws to back me up, and I had given the bartenders and waitresses clear instructions on how to deal with people who appeared intoxicated. It was business as usual and no big deal. Or was it?

"When I left the bar that night, Pat's unkind words were still ringing in my ears. Though I tried to put the incident aside, I found myself going back to it again and again. When I went to work two days later, I felt certain that Pat would 'see the error of his ways' and apologize. But Pat ignored me and continued to ignore me for the rest of the week.

"A week later, Pat asked me to come to his office and talked with me as if nothing had happened. I left Pat's office feeling somewhat relieved because we were talking again. But I was also confused, because Pat had clearly done something wrong, and he hadn't apologized or even referred to the incident. Why not?"

Finding Answers

For many months following, Tim thought about the incident. Why hadn't Pat apologized for his remark? Why did Pat ignore him for a week and then suddenly act as if nothing had happened? Why was Tim made to feel like a bad guy because he chose to do his job and comply with the law, a law that Pat was well aware of and seemed to support. Tim felt angry, frustrated, annoyed, vengeful, and stupid. Why was he still obsessed with the incident and Pat's treatment of him? The answers finally began to come to him during a lecture for adult children he attended.

"I began to realize that the boundary between Pat and I was fuzzy in terms of our relationship. Were we friends or employer/employee? Was it possible to be both? How could we set up our relationship so I wasn't confused when Pat was being a boss or when he was being a friend? The more I thought about it, the more I wanted and needed a firm boundary in place. I wasn't certain how to do that and knew the relationship would change, but I knew putting a boundary in place was necessary. Just identifying the problem was gratifying for me: I knew I was on the right track.

"I also realized that I had an intense fear of authority. I remembered how my parents treated me when they were drunk, and I began to see how I'd developed my people-pleasing habit. Of course, I was upset when Pat yelled at me. At home while I was growing up, my job was to keep the peace, and I still carried that sense of 'make peace at any cost.' "

This incident with Pat was similar to many in Tim's childhood when he thought he was doing "right" or "good," but found himself feeling embarrassed, ashamed, and defensive. Tim knew that he was close to lashing out at Pat and blaming him for his feelings of frustration. Instead, Tim called John, a friend from his support group, to discuss these feelings.

Tim and John talked a lot about *expectations*. Tim realized that he was expecting other people to change in the same way he was changing. Tim was expecting Pat to see how unfair he had been. Tim may not have been particularly nice when he said no to the customer that night, but Tim had done his job, a job that the law compelled all bartenders to do. Why had Pat been so negative about how Tim had handled it? Tim decided to get Pat's version of the story and was surprised by Pat's response.

"I'm a businessman, Tim," Pat had said. "I'm here to make money. You offended a customer with your moralizing and may have driven her away permanently. Sure, she'd had one too many, and you did the right thing by not serving her. But she didn't want or need a lecture, and you gave her one anyway. You need to learn to joke 'em through it. Driving them away means I lose customers and money. Lighten up."

Tim was expecting an answer that would mirror his sense of right and wrong—a value system. But Pat didn't have the same value system, nor did Pat like it when Tim shared his, especially with customers. Tim saw how he had set himself up for problems, despite his recovery program.

"I began, at that point, to learn when it is appropriate to speak up to Pat about my 'new' viewpoints and when it is appropriate to keep them to myself. By asking questions about how Pat viewed certain actions, I got direct information. I didn't have to play peacemaker anymore; I could be who I was. I also chose not to reveal anything more about my recovery program.

"In learning to check things out, I began establishing firm boundaries with Pat on several fronts. When I was working, Pat was my boss. When I was in the restaurant on my own time, or when the two of us were going to a social event together, we were friends.

"I worked very hard for over a year to try to establish the different boundaries with Pat. As usual, however, I was unprepared for some of the outcomes."

As Tim assessed his needs in his relationship with Pat, he saw that the relationship was changing direction: Tim discovered that understanding one's own needs and working to get them met is empowering. He also discovered that it takes two to make a relationship work, and Pat had no apparent interest in changing or accommodating some of the changes Tim requested.

Making Changes

Tim knew that the relationship was at a pivotal point and felt himself withdrawing. "The next six months were painful for me. I knew it was time to leave but found every reason or excuse to stay with my job. I went to more adult children's meetings, called friends to talk, read books, and even started karate classes, hoping to find release from the confusion and anger I felt. All these things were helpful, but the issue of my job and my relationship to Pat remained unsettled.

"Over time, I began to realize how my perfectionism made me unwilling or unable to take decisive action. I was trying to make the 'right' decision the 'right' way. Like most adult children, I thought I needed to learn the 'rules' about making transitions so that everything would turn out well for everyone concerned.

"But finally, I learned that the most successful, caring, and respectful way to make a change was to figure out what I wanted to do and then do it. Hanging on, hoping others would change, or hoping that the situation would change—all that would suffocate me emotionally, and that was the least perfect solution of all.''

Tim decided to leave his job. While off work, he decided to open his own bar and restaurant. Much to Tim's delight (and relief), Pat became one of his biggest supporters.

After two long, hard years, Tim's restaurant was up and running. Tim learned so much in the four years following the incident with Pat. ''It was one of the deepest and most meaningful experiences in my recovery program, and I'm grateful for it every day.''

Tim learned that his work issues were adult children issues: self-esteem, perfectionism, people pleasing, loyalty beyond reason, fear of the unknown, peacemaking, self-aggrandizement, and boundaries. He also learned to create choices for himself with his recovery skills. ''I chose to identify the issues in my relationship with Pat and do something about them. I assessed my value system and how and when I wanted to talk about it. I also discovered that not talking about some issues at certain times is a valuable choice that shows self-respect.''

In addition, he found that his loyalty to others and fear of ''rocking the boat'' kept him from getting his own needs met. The further he got in his recovery program, the less tenable it was for him to give away power and let others' decisions run his life. ''I discovered that I could support my decisions in the face of fear, loss, and anger. Nothing had turned out as I planned, yet everything, particularly my sense of myself and my abilities, had changed for the better.''

Tim's Mini Tune-up

Tim now feels able to establish appropriate boundaries with his employees. ''I understand how people pleasing and peacemaking-at-all-costs affect others. To keep my emotions manageable, I have created a 'mini tune-up' process designed specifically to adjust my attitudes at work.''

Every day, when Tim arrives at the office, he does three things. First, he looks over his business plan for the restaurant, reminding himself of his goals in terms of financial growth, employee relationships, a second restaurant, and so on. He then sets, for the day, some short-term objectives that support his long-term goals and ideals. He may work on new menu ideas one day, customer service the next. The main point is Tim is diligent, and each day he stays attentive to his goals and dreams. He doesn't get lost in crisis management, as he did so often in his childhood.

The second thing he does is review a list he created of what he likes to do outside of work—for example, going out with friends, practicing karate, taking his girlfriend to concerts, and attending Twelve Step meetings. Tim knows making his restaurant a success can require long hours of work every week. He also knows that to have the energy to run the restaurant, he needs to engage in activities where he can get his emotional needs met. "Otherwise I would look to work or my employees to meet those needs and would be frustrated," Tim says. Among other things, Tim designates one evening a week for entertainment and one for quiet time.

The third thing he does is read a meditation book specifically for adult children of alcoholics. The daily readings remind him of his recovery goals and that he isn't alone. "I need to remember that I'm not the only one who has coping problems and other troubles due to growing up in a dysfunctional family. Remembering that helps keep me from lashing out in frustration and helps me move to finding ways to cope with the situation."

The routine takes ten to fifteen minutes to go through. When he forgets it, or chooses to ignore it because of other tasks, his work attitude suffers and so do his employees. Tim likes its simplicity and how much it improves his days.

Cory's Story

I couldn't put him off or stop him from talking about uncomfortable subjects.

The third of eight children, Cory has known for many years that he wanted to be a builder, to work with his hands and his mind to create environments for people to live and work in. The son of a steelworker, Cory still lives in his hometown, which has had unemployment rates as high as 35 percent among the building tradespeople during the early 1980s. Though the local economy has improved in the last five years, many still fear what the future holds.

Cory had been managing a convenience store and attending class at a junior college. His dream of being able to save enough money to attend the state university in engineering was beginning to seem like just that—a dream. At twenty-three, Cory was, in many ways, just beginning to come to grips with the effects of being an adult child of an alcoholic. His family had gone through treatment for his mother's alcoholism when Cory was twelve. He had joined Alateen after the treatment program, and then changed to Al-Anon when he turned eighteen. Five of seven siblings and both parents regularly attend Twelve Step programs.

"When I first began the building apprenticeship program, I was surprised at how physically and mentally demanding the work was," he recalls. "Accustomed to learning things easily, I began having to put in overtime just to keep up. Even after nearly three months on the job, there were few things that I felt very confident about. My supervisor, Bud, was complimentary about most of my work, though, and I passed my tests on schedule. At least I knew I would probably be graduated into the second part of the training program. My friend and fellow apprentice, Robbie, wasn't so sure about his chances of moving on."

While Cory found the apprentice program rigorous, Robbie found it overwhelming. Slower at nearly everything than Cory or the other apprentices, Mick and Jim, Robbie struggled to keep up. Often, he put in overtime after a ten-hour shift, in the classroom and on the job. He even worked extra hours on Saturday to try to keep pace.

Though Robbie wasn't ready to move forward, Bud passed him into the second part along with the other three apprentices. To Bud, flunking him and having to teach him everything a second time was too much hassle.

"It was a long-standing ritual that when an apprentice passed to the second part of training, they were invited out after work with the rest of the crew," Cory says. "I was apprehensive about going to a bar; I had strong memories from childhood of looking for my mother and bringing her home when my father was 'out with the boys.' Just the smell of a bar was enough to set me off. I hoped to make up some excuse and leave after twenty minutes. Though I wanted to be a part of the group and knew that if I didn't show up there would be hell to pay, I thought it would be even more hellish to have to re-live painful memories for several hours.

"When Bud started to talk to me about Robbie's problems and asked my advice on how to deal with him, at first I felt flattered. Apparently, Bud thought enough of my opinion to seek it out. After a while, I became so engrossed in the conversation that I even lost my nervousness about being in a bar, or so I thought.

"When I finally left to go home, however, I began to feel funny about what I had said to Bud. If I was lucky, maybe Bud would forget what I said, and everything would go back to business as usual."

The problem, however, was just beginning. Feeling anxious when he saw Robbie the following day, Cory spent extra hours helping Robbie with a particularly difficult task. It was the start of a pattern for Cory. He decided to help his friend improve his skills, and he figured that Robbie would like the tutoring better if it came from Cory. Unfortunately, Cory never saw the connection between his conversation with Bud and his new protective feelings toward Robbie.

Over the next nine months, Bud continually sought out Cory's company. Bud talked to him not only about Robbie but about the other apprentices, the union, problems with general contractors, problems with Bud's boss, and so on. For some reason, Bud had chosen Cory, an apprentice eighteen years his junior, as his working hours confidant.

"After several months, I began to feel overwhelmed by Bud's intrusions. Though I tried to avoid situations where the two of us were alone, I often couldn't put him off or stop him from talking about uncomfortable subjects. I tried making jokes, changing the subject, and making excuses about having to leave, but no matter what, Bud would seek me out again.

"I was also feeling overwhelmed by Robbie's growing reliance on my tutoring. Finally, after nearly a year of listening to Bud and helping Robbie, often at the loss of my own study time and playtime, I lost control one night during a particularly ugly conversation with Bud, and I started yelling.

"Much of what I said was totally inappropriate. I called Bud names, was judgmental, crude, and unreasonable. Feeling trapped and unable to cope, I just lashed out at Bud, nearly becoming hysterical."

Bud was so incensed by Cory's outburst that he threatened to fail Cory on his next set of tests. Several weeks later, that's exactly what he did.

Dissecting the Problem

Cory called Joe, a friend from Al-Anon, the night of the fight. He knew that Bud was likely to make good on his threat of flunking him, forcing Cory to lose several months of work and credit. But he didn't know how to deal with his boss and still feel good about himself. His friend suggested that Cory dissect the problem with him to learn the source of the pain.

"The conversation that followed was one of those blinding flashes of the obvious for me," Cory said. After Cory described the situation, Joe agreed with him that Bud had been totally inappropriate many times. They agreed Bud had taken advantage of his position of power as Cory's boss and talked with him about things that were none of Cory's business, things that Cory felt compromised his friendship with Robbie, things that were illegal and should be told to a union official or a lawyer. The list went on and on.

Cory's real problem, they decided, was that he hadn't shared any of this with anybody. Bud, as his boss, could take advantage of the situation and harass Cory. Cory, however, didn't need to stay in the role of victim.

"I began to understand that I couldn't control my boss's behavior or go over his head and complain. If you rocked the boat in my union, you were continually blocked in your future attempts to secure work. I was no fool. I didn't want to compromise my future by talking with anybody in the union about my problems. But I could start talking with people in my group and others about my anger and frustration.''

Joe pointed out that Cory would have to decide whether he was willing to continue in his training program. ''I knew that Bud would make my life miserable if he could. I had already reached the end of my rope once, and wondered if I had the inner resources to keep putting up with the harassment.''

Finally, Joe pointed out that Bud probably wouldn't know that Cory didn't like the course of their conversations if Cory never told him so. Like Jim, the bartender, Cory was a peacemaker and people pleaser. Joe told Cory that, if he ever hoped to again be comfortable with his boss, he needed to learn to be assertive and tell Bud he didn't want to talk about some subjects. Cory needed to learn how to say no appropriately to his boss. The responsibility for the situation was as much Cory's as it was Bud's.

''It was a long time before I was willing to give up the victim mentality and start thinking about ways to empower myself. In the meantime, I continued with my training and finished the program three months after Robbie, Jim, and Mick. It was tough. Bud was as nasty as he could be, but I found other outlets for my frustration during this time and was able to graduate finally and become a journeyman carpenter—and Bud was no longer my boss.''

But Cory's problems weren't over yet.

''My first job as a journeyman was working for a general contractor who was building a new subdivision. Robbie had also been picked to work on this job. For several weeks, we were both so overwhelmed just trying to finish the work that neither of us had energy to do anything after work except go home. I'd been able to say no more often to Robbie when he asked for help, but I still struggled with the boundary between being a friend and doing my boss's job by training Robbie.

''After about a month on the job, I began to stop at the bar once in a while and talk with the other carpenters. I was beginning to feel like I belonged and was grateful to meet so many other people in construction. It helped hearing about all of the work being planned for the next year. I was beginning to believe that there might be enough work for everyone and that I would complete my training on schedule and become a full-fledged carpenter.''

Robbie decided to join Cory one night at the bar. Robbie's work had improved tremendously during the last week, and he was beginning to not only feel more confident about his work but to also be able to socialize more. He wanted to celebrate his improvement.

Robbie was more outgoing than Cory: wherever Robbie was, there was bound to be lots of fun. They were both feeling pretty good about their lives and their jobs that night. In addition to the group that was usually present, Bud had also stopped in.

Robbie immediately went over to Bud's table and started talking, excited to share his good news about the improvement in his work. Cory, on the other hand, felt embarrassed and out of place. Cory kept hoping that Robbie would come back and talk to him or at least go over to another table so he could join Robbie. An hour later, Robbie was still talking with the group at Bud's table, and Cory was feeling more and more angry and out of place. Cory finally went home, leaving Robbie, who was expecting a ride, behind.

"Robbie called that night wanting to know why I had left without telling him. He asked whether there had been a family emergency or if I had become ill. With real concern in his voice, he offered his assistance if I needed it.''

Cory, very upset and angry about Robbie's apparent disloyalty in talking to Bud for so long, started screaming and yelling. Robbie finally hung up.

Playing the "Victim" Role

As a person needing to come to grips with his childhood in an alcoholic family, Cory was still fighting several problems. First and foremost, Cory didn't trust people. He had imagined all sorts of terrible things that Robbie and Bud were talking about, including what an awful person Cory was. Cory just assumed the worst and left in a huff.

The second problem was Cory had created unreasonable expectations of his role as Robbie's friend and how Robbie should perceive him. When Robbie had gone over to talk to Bud, Cory felt Robbie had acted disloyally. Cory had spent hours helping Robbie in the last year, and his friend returned the favor by talking with their former supervisor, who Cory thought was a jerk. Throughout his tirade on the phone, Cory forgot that he had never told Robbie about his problems with Bud. And although Robbie knew there was tension between the two, he had no idea what had caused the tension.

The third part of the problem was that Cory had always felt badly about his early discussions with Bud about Robbie. Cory had known that it was wrong to gossip with his boss about anyone. Still, Cory hadn't dealt with his sense of shame about how shabbily he had treated his friend. Nor had he talked it through with anyone enough to know how he could begin to heal himself. He wanted to tell Robbie what had happened, but he wasn't sure that was such a good idea either. His secret was making him feel angry, sad, and confused.

Finding Valuable Help

The first thing Cory did was call his friend, Joe, again. Joe suggested that Cory attend several Al-Anon meetings each week instead of just one. If Cory believed that his behavior was the problem, then listening to other people with similar problems would probably be useful.

For the next year, Cory attended from two to four meetings a week. Instead of stopping at the bar after work, Cory stopped at the AA club for an Al-Anon meeting. He began to identify behaviors that got him into trouble. He also learned that, because of growing up in an alcoholic family, he was apt to use his old coping skills whenever he got in a situation where he felt trapped or scared. Basically, his defensive behavior was a bad habit that he was allowing himself to keep.

To help break the habit, Cory began attending a meeting specifically for people who had grown up in alcoholic families.

Cory listened to the introduction closely when the group leaders described common traits of adult children. He nearly laughed aloud at many of them because they so thoroughly described him. He hadn't ever met most of the people in the room, yet here they were describing him almost perfectly.

Cory felt at home from the very beginning. He learned about creating new habits and new ways of thinking. Best of all, he no longer felt so alone and isolated. He didn't automatically assume that he was a victim of circumstances when his boss criticized his work or when co-workers started gossiping about other crew members. He started thinking about his choices, and even if he couldn't stand up for himself on a particular subject, his new friends made good sounding boards for venting his frustration and pain.

One of the first things Cory wanted to work on was preventing his temper from having free rein when he was under pressure. When he practiced his new coping skills, he could do that. "It meant that I really could be in charge of myself the next time I felt 'under the gun.' "

When Cory learned several weeks later that Robbie had been talking about Cory whenever he could find a sympathetic ear, Cory created a plan. "It included calling Robbie and trying to make amends for my past behavior and seeing if we couldn't patch things up." Though Robbie accepted Cory's apology, he wasn't ready to try to be friends again. Cory took great satisfaction, however, in his willingness to call Robbie and apologize. Rather than trying to control Robbie's behavior or blame Robbie for being unreasonable, Cory took his pain at losing a friend and his shame for his past behavior to his new friends.

Cory's only complaint about his recovery program today is that it takes an incredible amount of time and effort to change old habits and learn new ones. He still thinks about moving to the city and going to night school in engineering at the state university. But, for now, he knows that he has more than he can handle just trying to keep himself on a forward path. It's frustrating at times, but Cory doesn't deny reality much anymore; he tries to think about his choices rather than about being a "victim."

Ellen's Story
I felt on top of the world and enjoyed myself thoroughly.

Ellen also had to learn about creating choices rather than feeling like a victim. At thirty-two, she was a salesperson in a company that creates business management seminars and presents them all over the world.

The daughter of alcoholic parents, Ellen had dropped out of college twice before graduating at age twenty-seven. At twenty-one, she dropped out when her father had died of cirrhosis of the liver. She dropped out again at twenty-four when her mother suffered a nervous breakdown and had been hospitalized for several months.

Although she had gotten a late start in her career, Ellen had moved steadily up the ladder, having been promoted four times in five years. She was currently working in the top sales division, traditionally a group from which new sales managers were chosen. She really liked her work and the people she worked with and for.

An ambitious, outgoing, and creative person, Ellen had long dreamed of being president of a training and development company similar to the one she worked for.

"I had always had something of a chip on my shoulder about my delayed finish of college. I had been devastated by my father's early death and really angered by my mother's lack of coping skills. I had worked extremely hard to 'make up for lost time' and was quite surprised when I became the youngest person in the top sales division."

Ellen had been in a grief therapy group for a year after her dad died and managed to stay in touch with several members of that group. "When my mother was hospitalized, my friends from that group were my staunchest supporters, helping me with the household tasks that I felt obligated to take over and offering a sympathetic ear. I had also joined Al-Anon after leaving therapy."

Ellen thought her office mates were a great group of people. Nearly everyone had been with the company for more than five years, unusual given the competitiveness of the sales industry.

In some ways, they were truly like Ellen's "dream" family: talented, ambitious, friendly, loyal, and fun. They worked well together and even had fun socializing occasionally on the weekends.

"Of all the sales management positions available in the company, my boss's was considered the 'plum.' Though I wanted to be a manager, I had never thought about my boss's job; several people in my department had more experience and seniority than me. When I heard that my boss had been promoted to vice president, I fully expected that either Bob or Theresa would get the job.

"When the senior vice president, Dick, called me that same afternoon, I was concerned. Had I done something wrong? Had one of my clients complained? Was I going to be fired?

"When Dick told me that he wanted me as the new manager, I was dumbfounded. I asked Dick several questions about when the promotion would be announced and when I could move into my new office. I just couldn't believe that I was going to be the next manager."

Ellen returned to her office and tried to collect herself and think about what she wanted to say to the group about her promotion. She gathered her wits as best she could, then asked the others to join her for an impromptu staff meeting. She then told her friends that she would be their new boss.

The reactions ranged from surprise to hearty congratulations to silence. Not surprisingly to Ellen, there was little reaction from Bob and Theresa. After offering good wishes to Ellen, everybody headed back to their offices.

When she got home, Ellen called her best friend, Susan. "I really wanted to go out and celebrate and asked Susan if she could join me. Susan was ecstatic about the great news and, rather than just the two of us going out that night, she wanted to throw a party for me and invite all of my friends, including those from work."

The party was scheduled for Saturday night. When Ellen announced it in her office, she was greeted with the usual hoots and howls that had always accompanied an invitation to a party in the old days.

"The party was a big success. More than forty people had shown up, many bringing me cards and gifts, offering congratulations, and saying how much I deserved the promotion. Almost everyone from the office had come except Bob. I felt on top of the world and enjoyed myself thoroughly. Everything seemed to be going just fine. Maybe my concerns about the others adjusting to me as manager were unwarranted."

The Crisis with Bob

The following day, a Sunday, Ellen moved her things into her new office. When she finished moving her files in, she sat down and started typing an agenda for the regular Monday morning staff meeting. The longer she worked, the more excited she became about incorporating new sales training methods and introducing new products. She wrote a short speech to deliver in the staff meeting and was starting to pack up when she heard a noise in the hallway and got up to investigate. It was Bob.

"Bob seemed surprised to see me there. After we chatted for a while, I screwed up my courage and asked Bob why he hadn't come to my party. Bob said that he hadn't gone to the party because he thought it would seem odd to celebrate my promotion, and then have to tell me that he was resigning. We talked for a long time about Bob's disappointment at being overlooked for promotion. He was forty years old, eight years my senior, and had been a top producing salesperson in the department for four years. He felt just plain ripped off by the senior management."

Ellen silently agreed with him that he hadn't been treated fairly and wished him the best of luck. She felt sad and angry, but knew she couldn't change his mind about resigning.

At home that night, Ellen vowed to try to create a more open atmosphere for communications in her department. Though she still had ultimate respect for Ruth, the previous manager, she wasn't very thrilled by Bob's story. If she could influence the future treatment of the employees in her department, she would do so.

The next day in the staff meeting, Ruth announced Ellen's

promotion and then went on about business. At the very end of the meeting, Ruth told the group that Bob had resigned effective immediately. She then announced that Theresa had also resigned and would be gone in two weeks. Ellen was shocked.

"After the meeting, I demanded an explanation for why Ruth hadn't told me before the meeting that Theresa was resigning. I was angered by Ruth's apparent lackadaisical attitude and offended by what I perceived to be a breach of protocol. Ruth, though, offered no real explanation, told me to relax, and headed off to another meeting. By the end of the day, I was feeling even more insecure and rageful at Ruth for what I considered patronizing treatment."

Two More Resignations

The first things that greeted Ellen Tuesday morning were two more resignations of very competent salespeople. Ellen panicked. Just five days before, she had thought of this job as being the best position in the company. Now she was faced with a major defection of four top-producing salespeople and a former boss who was uncommunicative and rude. Suddenly she was ready to give it all away. She got up, told her secretary to hold all of her calls, and closed the door. If she was going to fall apart, she was going to do it in private.

But she didn't fall apart. She called Susan instead. Ellen and Susan had eighteen years of recovery between them, eleven for Ellen and seven for Susan. They had been good friends for years and relied on each other's perspective and assistance. Ellen was scared that something else might go wrong and was saddened that her "dream family" was breaking up. She knew that her tendency was to blame others when she felt angry or frightened. After talking to Susan, however, she felt like she could at least get through the rest of the day.

The next six months were rough for Ellen. Sales figures dropped dramatically after Bob, Theresa, and the others had left. Ellen, continually embarrassed by having to report bad news at manager's meetings, felt isolated with her problems. Few people in the company, least of all Ruth, seemed interested in helping Ellen pull her department out of the slump.

Without some kind of miracle, Ellen's department would soon lose its status as being tops in the company, she thought. She was ashamed of acknowledging failure of any kind, and she was being immersed in it every day, it seemed. After a particularly frustrating week, Ellen decided that she would resign.

"I called Susan and, through tears, told her I was resigning. She invited me to her house so we could talk about what had happened.

"Richard, Susan's boyfriend, was there, and together we talked about my best course of action."

The Victim and Martyr Mentalities

"I went over to Susan's convinced that I'd finally made a good decision by being willing to leave my job. Nothing had worked out as I wanted, and I wanted to get out before everything fell apart. I was angry, sad, and exhausted from feeling alone with my problems."

When Ellen started to explain the situation to Richard, she found herself feeling even more rageful. How dare the company treat her and her department so poorly? She had been one of the most talented salespeople in her department, and management was acting as if she was the cause of the difficulties. Ellen went on and on about "them," blaming, projecting, feeling as if she had been victimized. Richard and Susan just let her talk until she finally felt finished.

Richard then asked Ellen what she hoped to gain by acting like such a victim. A recovering adult child of an alcoholic, Richard was only too familiar with the victim and martyr mentalities. In as kind a way as he could, Richard asked Ellen many questions about who was ultimately responsible for the problems Ellen was dealing with.

- Who was her boss? Her boss was Dick, not Ruth. Why was Ellen blaming Ruth for not doing a job that wasn't her responsibility?
- Why, if Ellen had hired four new experienced salespeople to replace those who had left, wasn't she doing everything she

could to train them and help them so that they could eventually be as good as the people whom they had replaced? And why, if she was having so many problems, wasn't she talking to her boss, Dick, at least every week if not every day? She really wasn't alone with the difficulties; it was as much Dick's responsibility as it was Ellen's. And if Dick didn't come to her office and offer help, then she had to seek him out.

Ellen had been presented with a lot of tough challenges, but feeling sorry for herself, not asking for help, and blaming her former boss probably weren't going to do anything more than get her deeper into trouble. It was time for a change of tactics.

"I was so surprised by Richard's assessment that I began to laugh. Even though I knew all of the self-help tools and had wonderful friends like Susan to support me, I plunged back into old behaviors with a vengeance when the going got tough. For a moment, I berated myself for not 'seeing it' earlier. Then I took a deep breath and asked Susan and Richard what they thought I should do."

With their help, Ellen created a plan that supported her emotionally and helped her to restructure her department and deal with setbacks. Richard suggested several books on management techniques that could help. Grateful to have a clear solution in mind, Ellen began to move forward again.

After another year and a half, sales levels in Ellen's department had finally gotten back to the same level as when Ellen had taken over. Other changes had occurred during those months, and Ellen was learning the true meaning of the word *acceptance*. She had wanted to be a superstar, to have everyone get along like one big, happy family, and to make innovative changes. But she learned that (1) she is a talented and capable manager, not a superstar; (2) people could be capricious and unfair in their treatment of her; and (3) few things turn out exactly the way you plan.

Ellen is thankful she didn't resign. She is finally accepting that it is enough that she do a good job and believe in herself.

She is grateful for the support of people like Richard and Susan.

Common Problems Adult Children Face at Work

These three stories point out common misconceptions and problems that adult children of alcoholics encounter at work. See if any of the following sound familiar to you:

Setting up inappropriate boundaries with bosses, colleagues, or subordinates. Tim, Cory, and Ellen all had difficulty relating to co-workers appropriately. Tim had to learn to deal with Pat in both the friend and boss roles.

Cory didn't know where his responsibility to his boss started or ended, and he didn't know how much help he was obligated to offer Robbie because of their friendship. Cory needed to clear up the blurred lines in those relationships to find peace for himself.

Ellen didn't know who to ask for help or that she could ask for help at all. Thinking of her co-workers as family created much frustration for her when they didn't act like loyal family members and left her department.

Having unrealistic expectations of co-workers, especially in terms of expecting them to act like recovering persons who share our value system. Tim expected Pat to "see the light" about not serving another drink to a customer who appeared to be intoxicated. That was clearly a value that Tim had created out of his recovery program. And he expected everybody around him to see the world through his new eyes. *Not so.*

Cory expected Bud would eventually understand the inappropriateness of talking with him about sensitive subjects. Cory had learned in recovery to let go of situations he couldn't control, but he hadn't learned how to say no or be assertive. He was expecting Bud to be the one to change. *Not so.*

It was Dick's responsibility to help Ellen with her new job.

She had to learn to ask for help from the right place and stop expecting to be "rescued."

Ellen thought that Ruth, her former boss, should help her even though that wasn't Ruth's responsibility. Ellen expected Ruth to act like Ellen's therapy group friends, who provided support when she needed it. *Not so, either.*

Creating win-lose, one-up, and one-down situations in the workplace instead of win-win situations. This is perhaps the most difficult issue to face. Most companies in America are based on hierarchical power structures. As you are promoted up the ladder, you gather power. This helps you beat the competition in the marketplace, or internally, if necessary. Bosses may have difficulty finding creative ways to deal with problems, or with motivation or discipline among staff. Workers may feel trapped by their inability to escape inappropriate disciplinary action or criticism.

Ellen wanted to remain friends with her staff even after she had been promoted to manager. She found it difficult to address issues with them because she wanted to maintain their old friendships instead of making the sometimes tough decisions that managers and leaders have to make.

Tim knew that his people-pleasing habits could get him into trouble with his employees and took extra care to address his own emotional needs outside the workplace in order to try to make good decisions in the restaurant. He still dislikes firing anyone, though, and he has to think hard about why.

Cory wanted Bud to rescind his failing grade on Cory's last set of tests. Cory also wanted Bud to see the inappropriateness in talking with Cory about sensitive subjects, but he didn't want to risk telling Bud to stop. Cory also wanted Robbie to agree that Bud was a jerk. In each case, Cory set himself up for failure because each scenario was dependent on someone else acting in just the right manner.

Win-win situations are really about goals, flexibility, and clear thinking. Cory could have "won" by asking for what he wanted in each case. If he had told Bud firmly and respectfully at the start that he didn't like talking about sensitive subjects, that would have been a strong win. It would have also created a win-win situation for Bud. If Bud had received clear, respectful messages from Cory, both would have avoided fighting with one another, and Bud would have had no reason to punish Cory. As it was, Bud was as trapped by Cory's fear as Cory was. Bud needed to know that there was a problem and to have the chance to respond.

Ellen could have created a win-win situation for herself, her employees, and her boss by creating a plan to move the department forward in spite of the losses in personnel. This may have entailed lowering sales projections or telling her boss right away about her need for help to solve the personnel problem. Ellen also could have created a win for all concerned by learning how to lead her staff instead of demanding that they act like her perfect family; this would have increased her confidence and skills. Ellen could also have "won" by creating a personal management style, rather than trying to graft Ruth's winning style onto herself.

Imposing our personal value systems on our work and on our fellow employees. Ethics in the workplace can be a hard issue for us because our value systems tend to occupy much of our awareness. Tim's value system was of top concern to Tim. And yet what right did Tim have to impose his value system on his boss, Pat, or the other employees or customers of the bar? For Tim to judge Pat as wrong because Pat's opinion was different than Tim's was just as much of an ethical breach.

In Cory's value system, extramarital affairs were immoral, so he had difficulty dealing with the subject when his boss, Bud, brought it up. And he didn't know whether to report what was just hearsay, or ignore it, when Bud told him about contractors taking illegal and dangerous shortcuts to keep from going over budget. Cory's father advised him that it was best to ignore what gossip he heard until he had actual physical evidence.

What about the many other unethical behaviors that some of us face every day? Cheating on taxes, exaggerating about product reliability, using inside information to make a killing on

Wall Street, stealing a co-worker's customer, telling little white lies to get out of work: ethical considerations are everywhere. We have choices to make about how we deal with our own value systems and how we learn to deal with others' values or corporate values that clash with our own.

No simple black and white answers exist. But you might consider talking with "safe people"—friends and sponsors, for example—before jumping into a situation that may test your values.

Using Power Reasonably

Most of us know a person who will do anything necessary to reach the top. Innumerable examples exist of businesspeople who have become millionaires with little concern for who or what they stepped on along the way. There are never-ending stories about politics and who is jockeying with whom for what position and who is winning. But many people who are in recovery lose the "killer instinct," the wish to deliberately harm others to get ahead themselves. We tend to harness our energies toward the work we engage in rather than "getting" other people. But we do need to learn to deal with power plays and to effectively use power that we have earned. To do this, we need to know ourselves, what our value systems are, and what kind of price we are willing to pay for acting differently.

Keeping all these concepts in mind while going about your job may seem overwhelming. But if you remember your goal— *finding a healthy balance*—you'll realize that you're probably intuitively employing these concepts in other areas of your life that are going well. Establishing a balance in the workplace, then, often becomes a matter of making good decisions when problems arise. We'll discuss how to sharpen these decision-making skills in the next chapter.

CHAPTER TWENTY-SIX

‖‖

Honing Your
Decision-Making Skills

Making decisions is usually one of the most difficult activities for adult children to engage in. Having come out of crises-oriented backgrounds and having dealt with mercurial, temperamental personalities in our families, we created numerous coping mechanisms. These often included delaying or deferring as many decisions as possible or becoming little dictators. Or we made decisions on anything and everything in our life as a way to exert control over our environment and stabilize the situation. If you live in a consistent state of crises, and most of us did as children, these aren't bad coping skills.

Shelley's Story
Too Little Rest, Too Much Fun, Strange Food . . .

Shelley took a trip to Florida when she was twenty-one with more than two hundred people from the same university. She was rooming with three other young women. They did the usual things that college students do during spring break in Florida: sat on the beach and got sunburned, ate strange food at strange hours, partied until the wee hours of the morning, then got up and did it again. Shelley and her friends had been there for a week and were packing up to leave on the last morning. All of them were tired. Two of her roommates had gotten up late and were moving around in the kitchen fixing themselves breakfast.

"Suddenly, Pam, one of my roommates, collapsed on the

floor and began having a seizure," Shelley recalls. "What none of us knew, but soon discovered, was that our friend was epileptic. The combination of too little rest, too much sun, and strange food had triggered the seizure. When Pam dropped to the floor, one of the other girls, Jill, began crying and was nearly hysterical. I jumped in and took control of the situation. My other roommate, Sally, moved the furniture immediately so that Pam would have less chance of injuring herself. I grabbed Jill and told her to calm down, find a phone book, call the front desk, and search for a doctor."

For the next two hours Shelley directed the decision making and came up with a solution to getting Pam home. She made plane reservations, informed the airline personnel of Pam's condition, and made sure that they could handle it if Pam had another seizure. She checked with a doctor to see how soon Pam could be moved, then called Pam's parents in Detroit and asked them to pick up Pam at the airport. Sally, the other levelheaded one, figured out where Pam could stay until the plane left; she called some people she had met in Florida who were staying nearby and asked them if Pam could rest in their room until she needed to go to the airport later that day. Less than two hours later, Shelley, Sally, and Jill were on a bus heading home.

Though on the surface this seems like a success story, and certainly parts of it are, the sad part for Shelley was that day-to-day decisions about school and work often felt totally overwhelming to her. For example, she often had a hard time making simple decisions like what to wear and where to study. She anguished over what classes to take, how to wear her hair, what her major should be, and whether to ask questions in her classes. Though she could obviously be counted on in a crisis, she had little sense of self-worth, purpose, or belonging. It was achingly painful for her to look in the mirror every day and know that the person other people apparently admired for "leadership qualities" felt like a miserable, scared, incompetent fake on the inside.

What Good Decision Making Means

Good solid decision making requires several things:

* information,
* input from others who will be affected,
* measurement of the risks of the possible outcomes of the decision, and
* a sense of the direction you are going.

Decision making also usually requires a cool head, patience, and a sense of humor. Most importantly, good decision making contains an aspect of detachment from the outcome. You may be chuckling to yourself, knowing that detachment is not a skill some adult children cultivate easily. But detachment is very important. If we attach a lot of importance to the results of a project and it fails, we start feeling like failures. If we wrap our self-esteem up in what happens and the project doesn't succeed, our self-esteem drops, depression and anxiety move in, and we begin to create even more problems because of our negative attitude. When we learn to detach from the outcome, we can look at a mistake, then step back and analyze the problem. We can discover where the mistakes were made and correct them, or we can change our expectations if they are too high. With detachment comes acceptance, serenity, and continued self-confidence rather than depression, failure, and a negative self-image.

Separating the Important from the Trivial

It is also important when making decisions to discern which ones are important (family, children, more expensive purchases, education) and which ones, though perhaps irritating, won't make a tremendous difference (decisions about what to wear, whether to wash the car, when to take down the Christmas tree). Though it seems like simple common sense to be able to separate the important from the trivial, it is common for us to stumble repeatedly and then become frustrated enough to make snap decisions. These usually prove to be only more negative and frustrating. Some insights follow on what can help. More of Shelley's story will provide a framework for these suggestions.

Shelley's Story Continued
I gained weight, complained a lot about small irritations . . .

After graduating from college, Shelley worked as a marketing manager for three years. Two years ago, Shelley left that job, which she adored, to further her career as a manager at a new company. Though at first the change was difficult, she felt challenged in her new position and supported by her old friends at her previous place of employment. She was also excited by all of the possibilities she saw in the new products and plans her present employer was creating. The future of this small entrepreneurial group seemed as brilliant and hopeful as any Shelley had encountered, and she felt privileged to have been given the opportunity to be part of it.

"For the first eight months, I was upbeat, future-oriented, hopeful, and full of the kind of energetic creativity associated with 'people on a roll.' From all appearances, I was feeling good about everything in my life, centered, happy, creative, and successful. Over the years, I often talked to my friends about the effects of my alcoholic parents on my life. But during this period it appeared that my recovery was successful and that I had found a way to live that was grounded, centered, and actively growing. One of my friends, Cindy, called work one day just before Christmas to invite me to a Christmas party. But I had left work early that day with a nasty headache. Cindy called again two days later, only to be told by my husband that I had a headache and couldn't come to the phone."

Shelley had been free of migraines for at least five years, so her friend was concerned. When Cindy called back on Friday of that week, however, Shelley was back to her cheerful, ebullient self. Shelley told her friend that she was fine and had just needed a couple of days off work to relax. When Cindy asked again if she was really okay, Shelley laughed, teased Cindy about hovering, and said again that she was great and stop worrying.

Over the next couple of months, Shelley became more and more distant, often sounding cheery on the phone but looking tired and even haggard in person. For the first time, her friends noticed that she was silent for hours even when surrounded by friends. On several occasions she didn't show up at parties, even though they were hosted by close friends who would welcome her no matter what mood she was in.

"There were other signs of distress too. I gained weight, complained a lot about small irritations that normally didn't affect me, and became short with Cindy over things that seemed small but which became fodder for arguments. Over the next six months, she spent less time with me. Cindy didn't know how to be friends anymore with someone who was apparently upset with her but who didn't express concerns or difficulties in a way that she could understand."

Nearly two years after Shelley had changed jobs, she called Cindy. Crying and nearly incoherent, she told Cindy that she had given notice on her job that day, that she had had enough and was leaving. Shelley had recently shared her frustrations about the people that she worked with, so it wasn't surprising to Cindy that she had chosen to leave. They talked for several hours about what had happened, the events that had led up to it, and what had finally triggered her decision. At the end of the conversation, Shelley sounded clearer and more decisive than she had in weeks. Though the anger and fear were still present, she had finally made a decision to leave and seemed to be moving forward again.

Shelley was to rescind and then remake the decision to leave her job dozens of times over the next several months. One day she thought she could stay. She would talk about the fact that it was still a wonderful opportunity and that she made a manager's salary and didn't think she could find another position that would pay her as much. The next day she was threatening to leave at the end of the week because she was so frustrated. Back and forth, back and forth, she hemmed and hawed. She cried and screamed and raged over the unfairness of it all, the pain of feeling like she had somehow failed, and her fear of not having enough money to pay the bills. Having grown up with parents who were both regularly unemployed, Shelley had a deep fear of ending up as homeless, living off of other people's handouts.

This experience clearly outlines how much fear and pain can drive the decision making of adult children. If you believe that Shelley was simply lacking in knowledge about how to deal with her background, she is a woman with years of both individual and group therapy behind her. She has eight years in a Twelve Step recovery program, a loving husband, and a close group of friends, many of whom are in recovery programs of one type or another. Although she had done many of the things recommended in this book for a very long time, she was still in intense pain about a situation in her life about which she felt unable to find distance and perspective.

What Shelley Did About Her Problem

After several months of back and forth, Shelley began to see what was happening to her because of the fear that was driving her.

- She began to accept her fear of lack of money and started to work with her husband to plan budgets for the next several months.
- She again began to keep a journal regularly and found it an excellent way to organize her thoughts and detach from the problem. Journaling also, in her words, "cut the monsters down to manageable size." She could edit, delete, or throw out pages or passages that didn't fit her script for the future.
- She began to visualize how she could succeed with her decision to change.
- She was able to find a sponsor and made a contract to call her once a week or more for three months.
- She wrote several affirmations and taped them to her bathroom mirror and her refrigerator to remind her to think well and clearly.

• When she talked to her close friends, they made a contract to talk about the blessings in their lives rather than their problems. They talked about "opportunities to grow" rather than playing the old "woe is me" game.

All these steps helped Shelley take the pressure off herself and delay her decision whether to stay or leave until she sensed she was thinking clearly and had dealt with her fears about the future. When she finally decided to leave her position, she knew why she was leaving. More importantly, she knew where she was going and where to find love and support while she secured another position. After five months, she found another job.

This story clearly outlines how adult children are sometimes paralyzed by fear, anxiety, people pleasing, perfectionism, and shame, which is one of the hardest emotions of all to identify.

Clear Thinking=Good Decision Making

So how can we, in the course of daily living, stay clear enough about what we want to make good decisions? Shelley's story offers several approaches that are useful.

1. *Identify the issues that you are dealing with.*
Sounds simple enough, doesn't it? Just identify the issue that you are dealing with and you've got a good start on the problem. But looking at Shelley's story, what was the issue she was dealing with? Was it trying to leave a job she didn't like? Was it not asking for help often enough? Was it being afraid of ending up homeless? Was it perhaps all of the above?
The problems or issues in our lives have layers to them much like the layers of an onion. We identify an issue as *the* root cause of a problem in our life, only to discover later that it was just an outer layer of a deeper issue. Shelley discovered that the problem was she didn't like her job. The other issues that came into play were that

- she was terrified of being without an income,
- she didn't talk about her problems often enough and thus built up layer upon layer of frustration, and
- her self-care program needed a tune-up.

She painfully discovered these layers. Many "big" issues are multi-layered, and it takes time to identify the layers.

2. Know what you want when making a decision.

You may say, "It is true that I need to know what I want, but if I knew what I wanted I would make a decision, and this whole process would be all done! So how can I find out what I *really* want?"

As she was vacillating, Shelley figured out that she essentially didn't know what she wanted. She then took herself off the emotional roller coaster and began to figure out which tools would be of use to her to gather the information she needed. She started by asking herself what she really wanted and then made the following list:

- I want several people in my life to pay close attention to me for several weeks.
- I want to act responsibly to my employer, to my family, and to myself.
- I want to figure out whether I have enough money to just quit or whether I need to wait until I can secure another position.

Shelley took herself off the hook when she realized that she couldn't make a decision under her present circumstances. She made a decision to back off and take time to think and plan.

3. Give yourself enough time and information, but don't dally out of fear.

You may say, "If I ever had time, I'd get the information I needed, and I wouldn't put decisions off because I'd have enough information, right?" Yes, all too true, but you must ask yourself how much is the delay caused by laziness, procrastination, or simply lack of time? If you're being lazy, you can ask yourself, *How important is this for me?* And then take action. If you're procrastinating, you can ask yourself, *Why?* Are you afraid of something? Are you feeling pressured and not responding because of authority issues? Did you say yes to doing something when you meant no? Answering these questions will help you gather the information you need, sort through it, talk over your concerns, and then move on. If you find that you ''don't have enough time,'' figure out how to make time because there is always time for what's important to you. Otherwise ''not enough time'' is just an excuse to delay or defer.

4. *Record the possible outcomes of your decision.*

When we take time to think about the possible consequences of a major decision, we can often see the ramifications. If the risks are acceptable for either the positive or negative outcomes, we can go ahead and take action. Though Shelley's decision-making process broke down long before this, she got into particular trouble because she didn't think through the ramifications of leaving her job. She discovered early that the risks were too high and therefore unacceptable. She backed off making a decision until the risks of taking action were more acceptable.

MAKING A LIST OF POSSIBLE OUTCOMES

On a separate sheet of paper,

1. Make a list of things you want in your life.
2. Next to each item, write what you think are the possible outcomes if you pursued what you want.

This way, you can decide what's important to do or not to do. Then you can decide what you really want and go after it.

It's probably a good idea to keep your lists for a while. If one of the outcome factors changes, and things can change rapidly, you are 90 percent of the way to making a good, measured, informed decision if you can simply grab this worksheet and redo just one or two segments of it. You are well on your way to taking advantage of a situation with a "small window of opportunity" this way—without having to make a poorly informed decision under pressure.

One Last Thing About Decision Making . . .

Remember to exercise a sense of humor at least as often as good judgment. We adult children are often so serious that we forget to laugh, play, and enjoy ourselves.

It also may be a good idea to pray about things. Even making big decisions can be fun, if we remind ourselves of the joy of living through laughter and prayer. Instead of thinking critically of ourselves when we make a mistake, we can laugh about it with those who love us. And detach, detach, detach from the outcome. We'll achieve our goals when we can get out of our own way!

PART FIVE

Hanging in There

CHAPTER TWENTY-SEVEN

The Art of Persistence

Perhaps you remember the story of the two frogs who fell into the pail of cream. The first frog paddled furiously in the cream, soon exhausted itself, gave up, and drowned. The second frog paddled furiously at first, then slowed its exertions, but kept paddling all the same. It did not give up, remained hopeful, and eventually hopped out of the pail when the cream it was churning turned to butter.

The art of persistence is very much like churning cream into butter. Sometimes you can churn and churn but see no sign that butter is forming. Then all of a sudden, in a magic moment, the cream thickens and butter begins to form. It's rather like the process of whipping egg whites to a stiff consistency, or stirring the ingredients that will eventually result in a cream sauce. It's necessary to keep whipping or stirring, even though the eventual outcome is not readily apparent from the initial lengthy efforts.

The tenacity of old behavior and patterns can be awesome. And sometimes just when you think you've gained some awareness and made progress, an event, conversation, or activity will trigger reactions, thoughts, and behavior that you thought you'd overcome. When that happens, you may tend to feel angrier and more upset with yourself because you "knew better," and you should have done it differently. Does the thought ever cross your mind that awareness can be more of a curse than a blessing? And do you then feel guilty for even letting that thought enter your mind?

You are *not* alone.

The progress we make in our recovery is never straight forward. It zigs and zags, stays in one place for a while, leaps forward, and hopscotches backwards. We must give ourselves some peace, patience, and understanding as we follow the path of recovery. After all, we practiced these behaviors and thought patterns for years. Is it any surprise that we're *very* good at them? As writer and counselor Earnie Larsen has remarked, "Recovery is simple, but not easy."

Phyllis' Story
The Internal Battlefield

During a recent three-day holiday weekend, Phyllis went to an inspiring and beautiful church service with a dear friend and talked to another friend on the phone several times. But because Phyllis was taking a computer class, she allocated a great deal of time that weekend for working on a computer program.

Although Phyllis patted herself on the back because she'd accomplished a great deal, she spent a good part of one day deep in the blues. She was angry, frustrated, and puzzled about the fact that Jake, a man she'd been dating for two months, hadn't asked her out when they'd talked the week before. She found her thoughts spiraling to the endless "chatter" that seems to always be present under these circumstances: *Did I say something wrong or do something wrong? . . . Maybe I was too enthusiastic or talked too much about myself . . . Has he been seeing somebody else? . . . I wonder what she has that I don't? . . . Would it be okay to call him since he called me last? . . .* And on and on . . . you get the picture. Letting go when warfare is waged on this internal battlefield can be one of the most difficult things to do.

Even though Phyllis wrote her feelings in her journal and tried relaxation exercises, nothing seemed to calm the battle raging in her mind. Finally she decided she needed to verbalize her frustration and called a good friend. Phyllis complained bitterly, vented her frustration, and listened as her friend raged about a few things happening in her life. By the end of the conversation, they felt very relieved and managed to laugh at themselves. Thank God for friends!

"I'm trying not to be too hard on myself for wallowing in old patterns," Phyllis says. "I realize that I will always be especially vulnerable around relationship issues. So my only recourse is to accept hurt feelings and disappointment, try a variety of techniques to defuse the situation, and then determine what it is that I'm not getting and if there's any way to get it. After I'd talked to my friend, I found that repeating affirmations and reading an inspirational book helped me get back toward center.

"After that, I went to my desk and plunged into studying for the class I was taking. This all helped, but it wasn't until three days later when I called Jake to check out what was going on that I really felt a sense of empowerment. I finally reached a point of not being willing to spend time worrying and decided to face the situation directly. In the two and a half hour conversation, Jake and I had brought up some issues that would never have occurred to me alone—issues relating to needs we had in the relationship. Both of us wanted to continue seeing each other. And there was an added bonus: Jake said that he felt closer to me after our discussion."

Many people in recovery agree that realizing that "this too will pass," even though it's painful at the moment, can sometimes be consoling. Also realizing that we have no control over others' actions, but only over our own attitudes and behaviors, can give us a sense of understanding. We can choose to realize that we give our own power away when we let ourselves feel helpless. We can concentrate instead on what we want for our lives and then take action to move forward in reaching one of our goals.

Persistence sometimes means plodding and not plunging forward. It sometimes means trusting that there is light ahead even though it is pitch dark at the moment. Persistence may seem boring, unrewarding, and uneventful. But just one of the efforts, however small, may be enough to spark a new direction, set a new course, or create a new condition. And that new direction, new course, or new condition may be what makes the difference. We never know exactly how it will develop; we just need to trust that it will.

Epilogue

Persistence in bettering our lives and putting one foot in front of the other in a mindful, conscious way is what recovery is all about for adult children. We will always meet new challenges along this path. And though sometimes we may despair of ever being truly free of the codependency patterns that have permeated our lives, one final story from the authors may offer hope.

During the three years of writing this book, we had two disagreements. Both disagreements were short and dealt with quickly when we recognized that one or the other of us was being unreasonable. It had become obvious to us after the first year that we were committed to what we were doing. What was less obvious was that we would need to use our recovery skills constantly to keep the process running at all, let alone smoothly.

The authors of this book have different personalities, not surprisingly. Sheila tends to be extroverted and temperamental; Elise is introverted and is apt to withdraw when she feels down. We both struggle with feelings of insecurity and, because of that, we are both known to swing from high to low quite rapidly when our egos get involved. We set our expectations too high only to have them dashed.

Both of us worked full time in management capacities while we wrote this book. We also taught part time, are home owners, and have the usual number of friends and social commitments including some volunteer work. One of us changed jobs during this three-year period; one of us ended a significant relationship and began another.

We have endured financial, emotional, and physical hardships, some of which proved to be among the most significant lessons we believe we will live through in our lifetimes. The beauty of it for us—and something that we are grateful for—is that, despite hardships, we put our energy where our thoughts were and worked our recovery programs while writing about them as well.

We saw that when we managed our own negative personality traits, we found how complementary our work could be. We learned to bring out the best in each other and support each other rather than fling blame or anger when we felt low or scared or panicked about a deadline. During times when it would have been only too easy to slip back into codependent or reactive behaviors, we tried to remember to talk things out instead. Or we agreed to put things on the back burner until we could be more present and offer constructive ideas and solutions.

Two disagreements over the course of three years on a project as major as writing a book reflect progress and hope. We have had the privilege of seeing our own movement and personal growth and recording some of it, and we believe beyond a shadow of a doubt that the techniques found in this book work. Our friendship, our sanity, and this book are living proof.

Can you rewrite old, negative thought patterns to change your future scripts? Instead of feeling trapped in the cycle of fear, can you break out of helplessness and move your life forward?

The answer is a resounding yes. You can do it. That's not to say it's easy. It's not. But you're worth it. You *can* learn better coping mechanisms that free you from feeling caged and hopeless. You can meet and deal with your fears in a spirit of openness and adventure. You can ask for guidance in living each moment to the best of your abilities.

We hope some of the ideas and techniques presented in *Creating Choices* have given you more options, more good raw materials for your new self. With more options comes a greater sense of personal empowerment and responsibility. And with a sense of personal empowerment and responsibility comes the ultimate joy of freedom—the freedom to create a life that fulfills your dreams.

Endnotes

CHAPTER THREE
Developing Purpose

1. Gail Sheehy, *Pathfinders* (New York: Bantam, 1981), 13–22.
2. Richard Leider, *The Power of Purpose* (New York: Ballantine Books, 1985), viii.
3. Ibid., 70
4. Ibid., 45.
5. Ruth Ross, *Prospering Woman: A Complete Guide to Achieving the Full, Abundant Life* (San Rafael, Calif.: Whatever Publishing), 123–26.
6. Ibid., 134–38.
7. Ibid., 138–40.
8. Ibid., 118–20.
9. Susan Fowler Woodring, "Goal Setting For Professionals" (Careertrack Seminar, 1986). Reprinted with permission of Careertrack, 1-800-334-6780.

CHAPTER FOUR
Developing Your Goal-Setting Process

1. James Newman, *Release Your Brakes* (Costa Mesa, Calif.: HDL Publishing, 1988).
2. Michael LeBoeuf, *Imagineering: How to Profit from Your Creative Powers* (New York: Berkley Books, 1980), 29.
3. Ibid., 31.
4. Ibid., 37.
5. Ibid., 31–32.

CHAPTER THIRTEEN
Mindfulness: Creating an Attitude of Joy
1. Joan Borysenko, *Minding the Body, Mending the Mind* (Reading, Mass.: Addison-Wesley, 1987), 112–13.

CHAPTER SEVENTEEN
Understanding and Appreciating Synchronicity
1. Carl Jung, *Synchronicity: And a Causal Connecting Principle,* translated by R. F. C. Hull, Bollingen series, vol. 20 (Princeton, N.J.: Princeton University Press, 1973), 5.

CHAPTER EIGHTEEN
Introduction to Guidance Mechanisms
1. Herbert Benson and William Proctor, *Your Maximum Mind* (New York: Random House, 1987), 30.

CHAPTER TWENTY
Understanding and Using Subliminal Techniques
1. Susan Smith Jones, *Choose to be Healthy* (Berkeley, Calif.: Celestial Arts, 1987), 52–53.

CHAPTER TWENTY-TWO
Incorporating Visualization Techniques into Your Life
1. James Newman, *Release Your Brakes!* (Costa Mesa, Calif.: HDL, 1988).
2. Ibid.
3. Ibid.

CHAPTER TWENTY-THREE
Using Affirmations to Break Old Patterns
1. Susan Jeffers, *Feel the Fear and Do It Anyway* (New York: Fawcett Columbine, 1987), 74–76.

Select Bibliography

Benson, Herbert, and William Proctor. *Your Maximum Mind.* New York: Random House (Times Books), 1987.

Borysenko, Joan. *Minding the Body, Mending the Mind.* Reading, Mass.: Addison-Wesley, 1987.

Jeffers, Susan. *Feel the Fear and Do It Anyway.* New York: Fawcett (a division of Ballantine Books/Random House), Columbine, 1988.

Jung, Carl G. *Synchronicity: And a Causal Connecting Principle.* Translated by R. F. C. Hull. Bollingen series, vol. 20. Princeton, N.J.: Princeton University Press, 1973.

LeBoeuf, Michael. *Imagineering: How to Profit from Your Creative Powers.* New York: Berkley Books, 1986.

Leider, Richard J. *The Power of Purpose.* New York: Ballantine Books, 1985.

Newman, James W. *Release Your Brakes!* Costa Mesa, Calif.: HDL, 1988.

Ross, Ruth. *Prospering Woman: A Complete Guide to Achieving the Full, Abundant Life.* San Rafael, Calif.: Whatever Publishing.

Sheehy, Gail. *Pathfinders.* New York: Bantam Books, 1982.

Index

A

Action, taking, 50–51
Adult Children of Alcoholics
(Woititz), 20
Affirmations, 161–63
  finding right affirmations, 161–63
  negative-positive technique, 167
  tips on using, 164–65
  what we desire is already in our
    lives, 163–64
Aha experiences, 145–46
Anxiety reduction, 149
Approval-seeking behavior, 62–63
Asking for what you want, 104–9
  getting started, 112–13
  getting the most out of life,
    exercise for, 112

B

Benson, Herbert, 136–37
Black, Claudia, 20
Buscaglia, Leo, 94–95

C

Causality, 120
Centeredness, 26
Choices, process of creating, 91–
  95
Commitment, cultivating a sense
  of, 79–82
Connectedness to Higher Power,
  25–26

Conscious mind, 143
Coping strategies, 32
Cousins, Norman, 4
Creative Visualization (Gawain), 163

D

Deadline setting, 54
Decision-making skills, 200–1, 203–
  6
  clear thinking and good
    decision making, 206–8
  good decision making, 202
  laughter and prayer, 209
  list of possible outcomes, 209
  separating important from
    trivial, 202–3
Direction, finding sense of, 33–36
*Do What You Love, The Money
  Will Follow* (Sinetar), 31
Dreams, tapping subconscious
  through, 146
Dysfunctional family, 32

E

Edison, Thomas, 145
Exercise, 138–41

F

Favorite place, getting in touch
  with, 43–44
Feel the Fear and Do It Anyway
  (Jeffers), 162–63

Fight or flight response, 149
Flexibility, 54

G
Gawain, Shakti, 163
Goal-setting process, 48–50
  exercises for, 53–55
  and flexibility, 54
  imagining attainment of goal, 55
  prioritizing goals, 53–54
  realistic goals, 54
  risk taking, 52
  setting deadlines, 54
  taking action, 50–51
Guidance mechanisms, 133–37

H
Hagberg, Janet, 93
High expectations, 71–74
High expectation syndrome, 73
Humor, 4

I
Imagineering (LeBoeuf), 49
Inner child, listening to, 29–30
In Search of Excellence (Peters
     and Waterman), 34
Intuition, 96–100
*Inventurers: Excursions in Life
     and Career Renewal, The*
     (Leider and Hagberg), 93
It Will Never Happen to Me
     (Black), 20

J
Jeffers, Susan, 162–63
Journaling, 169–72
Jung, Carl, 119, 120
Justice, Blair, 150

K
Keller, Helen, 52
Kennedy, John F., 49

L
LeBoeuf, Michael, 49, 53

Leider, Richard, 34, 93
Life purpose statement, 46
Lincoln, Abraham, 101
Living mindfully, 29

M
Martyr role, 194–96
Maslow, Abraham, 9
Meditation, 148, 153
Mindfulness, 101–3, 123–24

N
Negative-positive technique, 167
Negative thinking, 58–59, 149–50
Newman, James W., 48, 156, 158

O
Only Diet There Is, The (Ray), 140

P
Pareto Principle, 54
Past life, tapping into, 42–43
Pathfinders (Sheehy), 34
Patience, 3
Persistence, 213–16
Peters, Thomas J., 34
Power of Purpose, The (Leider),
     34
Proctor, William, 136
Professional help, 12
Project, starting, 59–60
Prospering Woman (Ross), 35
Purpose, 27–28, 46
  determining what we like to do,
     31–33
  finding sense of direction, 33–
     36
  getting in touch with favorite
     place, 43–44
  identifying your values, 36–39
  life purpose statement,
     developing, 46
  self-discovery exercises, 40–42
  tapping into past life areas of
     inner joy, 42–43
  Values Quiz, 37–39

R

Ray, Sondra, 140
Recovery resources, 7–9, 13–22
  decision-making criteria about
    recovery, 22–23
  other resources, 13
  professional help, 12
  recovery process, 9–12
  rigid thinking, avoidance of, 10
  support groups, joining, 10–12
Relaxation:
  anxiety/stress reduction, 149
  benefits of, 148–49
  interrupting negative thought
    patterns, 149–50
  listening to tapes, 152–53
  sense of control in our life, 150
Release Your Brakes! (Newman),
  48, 156
Reward system, designing, 83–87
Right brain thinking, 42–43, 136
Rigid thinking, avoiding, 10
Risk taking, 52
Ross, Ruth, 35

S

Self-actualizing, 9–10
Self-discovery exercises, 40–42
Self-esteem, 56–57, 60–62,
  65
  being true to ourselves, 62–63
  negative thinking, stopping
    cycle of, 57–58
  negative thoughts, replacing
    with positive affirmations,
    58–59
  starting a project, 59
Sheehy, Gail, 34
Sinetar, Marsha, 31
"Six-Month Want List," 95
Slippery situations, 75–78
  planning ahead to circumvent,
    77–78
Spirituality:
  and centeredness, 26

Power, 25–26
  developing, 28–30
  listening to our inner child, 29–30
  living mindfully, 29
  personal definition of, 24–25
  and purpose, 27–28
Stress reduction, 149
Subconscious mind, 143
  and aha experiences, 145–46
  empowerment through, 143–44
Subliminal techniques, 142, 147
  aha experiences, 145–46
  and conscious mind, 143
  empowerment through
    subconscious, 143–44
  and subconscious mind, 143
  tapping subconscious through
    dreams, 146
"Success Cycle," 49–50
Support group, 10–12
  in metropolitan areas, 11–12
  in rural areas, 11
Survival strategies, 32
Synchronicity, 86, 119–23, 124–26
  practicing mindfulness, 123–24
  Synchronicity (Jung), 120

T

Taking responsibility for
    ourselves, 66–70
Trusting in the outcome, 114–18

V

Values, identifying, 36–39
Values Quiz, 37–39
Victim role, 187–88, 194–96
Visualization techniques, 154–55
  benefits of, 155–56
  experience vs. observation, 157
  important things to remember,
    157–58
  practicing visualization, 160
  specific techniques, 159

W

Waterman, Robert H., Jr., 34

Watt, James, 145
Who Gets Sick (Justice), 150
Woititz, Janet, 20
Workplace, recovery in, 175–77,
    180–82, 196–99
  common problems adult
    children face at work, 196–99
  dissecting the problem, 185–87
  finding answers, 178–80
  finding help, 188–89

making changes, 180–81
playing the ''victim'' role, 187–
    88
using power reasonably, 199
victim and martyr mentalities,
    194–96

Y
Your Maximum Mind (Benson and
    Proctor), 136–37

About the Authors

Sheila Bayle-Lissick has served as Marketing Director for a research and development group benefitting children and their families and as Representative for Development and Marketing Services with a public television station in Minnesota. Bayle-Lissick is pursuing a B.S. degree in Marketing Education from the University of Minnesota.

Elise Marquam Jahns is Manager, Planning and Development with a public television station in Minnesota, and is a part-time instructor at two community colleges. Marquam Jahns has an M.A. degree in English from Cleveland State University.

Bayle-Lissick and Marquam Jahns teach a popular college class called "Creating Choices: Getting What You Want," that focuses on setting and achieving goals.

"EASY DOES IT BUT DO IT"
with Hazelden Recovery Books

THE 12 STEPS TO HAPPINESS *by Joe Klaas*
36787-1 $4.95

BARRIERS TO INTIMACY: For People Torn by Addictive and Compulsive Behavior *by Gayle Rosellini and Mark Worden*
36735-9 $4.95

BACK FROM BETRAYAL: A Ground-Breaking Guide To Recovery For Women Involved With Sex Addicted Men *by Jennifer Schneider, M.D.*
36786 $4.95

LIVING RECOVERY: Inspirational Moments for 12 Step Living *by Men and Women in Anonymous Programs*
36785-5 $4.95

COMPULSIVE EATERS AND RELATIONSHIPS *by Aphrodite Matsakis, Ph.D.*
36831-2 $4.95

These bestsellers are available in your local bookstore, or order by calling, toll-free 1-800-733-3000 to use your major credit card.

Price and order numbers subject to change without notice. Valid in U.S. only.

For information about the Hazelden Foundation and its treatment and professional services call 1-800-328-9000. In Minnesota call 1-800-257-0070. Outside U.S. call (612) 257-4010.